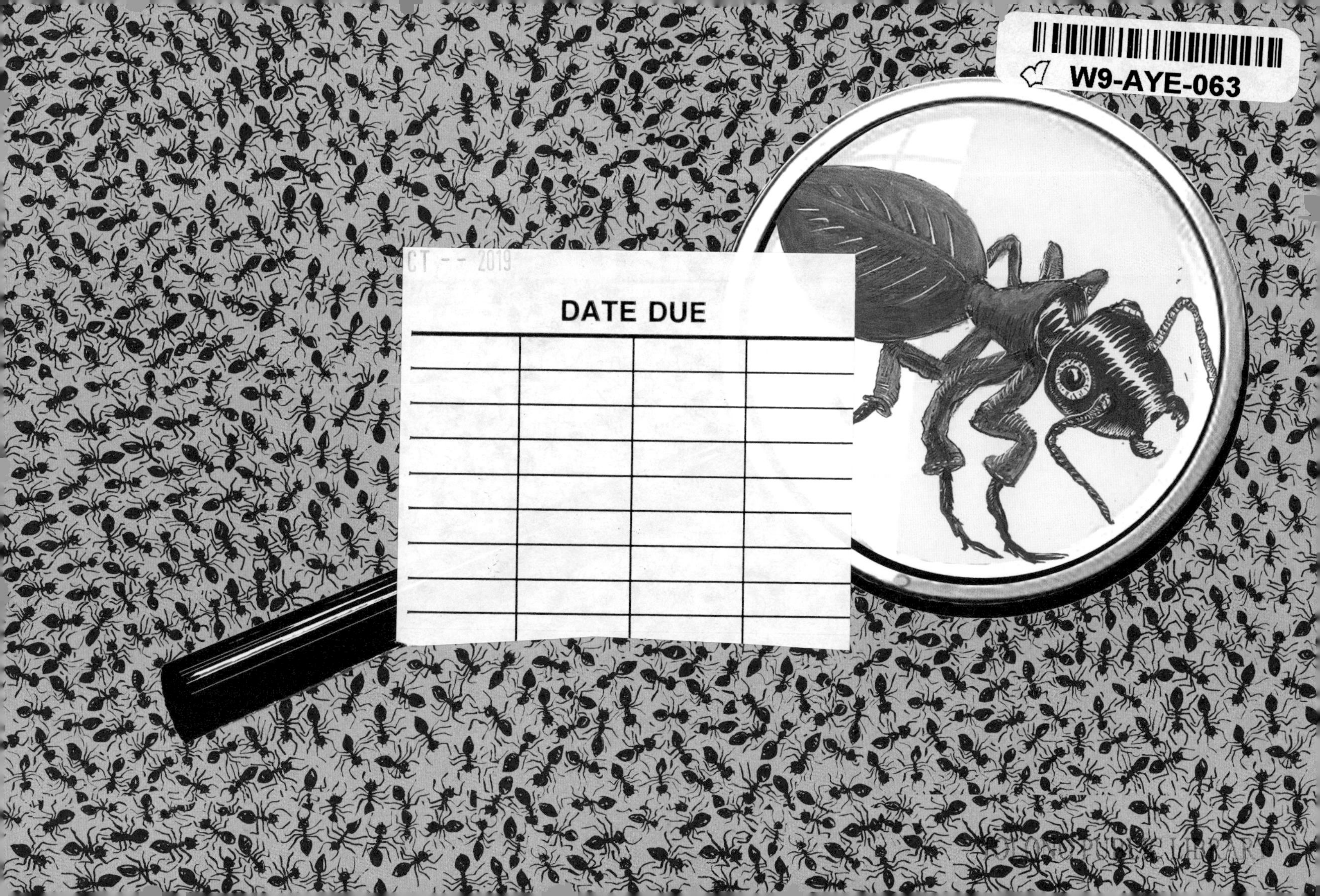

For the children who teach me things, like Francie at the Takoma Park Maryland Library who told me about **EXPLODING ANTS!**

(jlg) GOLD STANDARD

A JUNIOR LIBRARY GUILD SELECTION

Look for other *Giggle and Learn* books:
WE DIG WORMS!
THE REAL POOP ON PIGEONS!
SOMETHING'S FISHY!
SNAILS ARE JUST MY SPEED!
by the same author

Editorial Director & Designer: FRANÇOISE MOULY

KEVIN McCLOSKEY'S artwork was painted with acrylics and gouache on recycled paper bags.

A TOON BOOK

Library of Congress Cataloging-in-Publication Data: Names: McCloskey, Kevin, author, illustrator. Title: Ants don't wear pants / Kevin McCloskey. Other titles: Ants do not wear pants Description: New York, NY : Toon Books, an imprint of RAW Junior, [2019] | Series: Giggle and learn | Audience: Age 3+ | Audience: K to Grade 3. Identifiers: LCCN 2019009186 | ISBN 9781943145454 (hardcover) Subjects: LCSH: Ants--Juvenile literature. | Ants--Behavior--Juvenile literature. Classification: LCC QL568.F7 M3845 2019 | DDC 595.79/6--dc23 LC record available at https://lccn.loc.gov/2019009186

All our books are Smyth Sewn (the highest library-quality binding available) and printed with soy-based inks on acid-free, woodfree paper harvested from responsible sources. Printed in China by C&C Offset Printing Co., Ltd. Distributed to the trade by Consortium Book Sales & Distribution, a division of Ingram Content Group; orders (866) 400-5351; ips@ingramcontent.com; www.cbsd.com

ISBN: 978-1-943145-45-4 (hardcover)

19 20 21 22 23 24 C&C 10 9 8 7 6 5 4 3 2 1

w w w . TOON-BOOKS . com

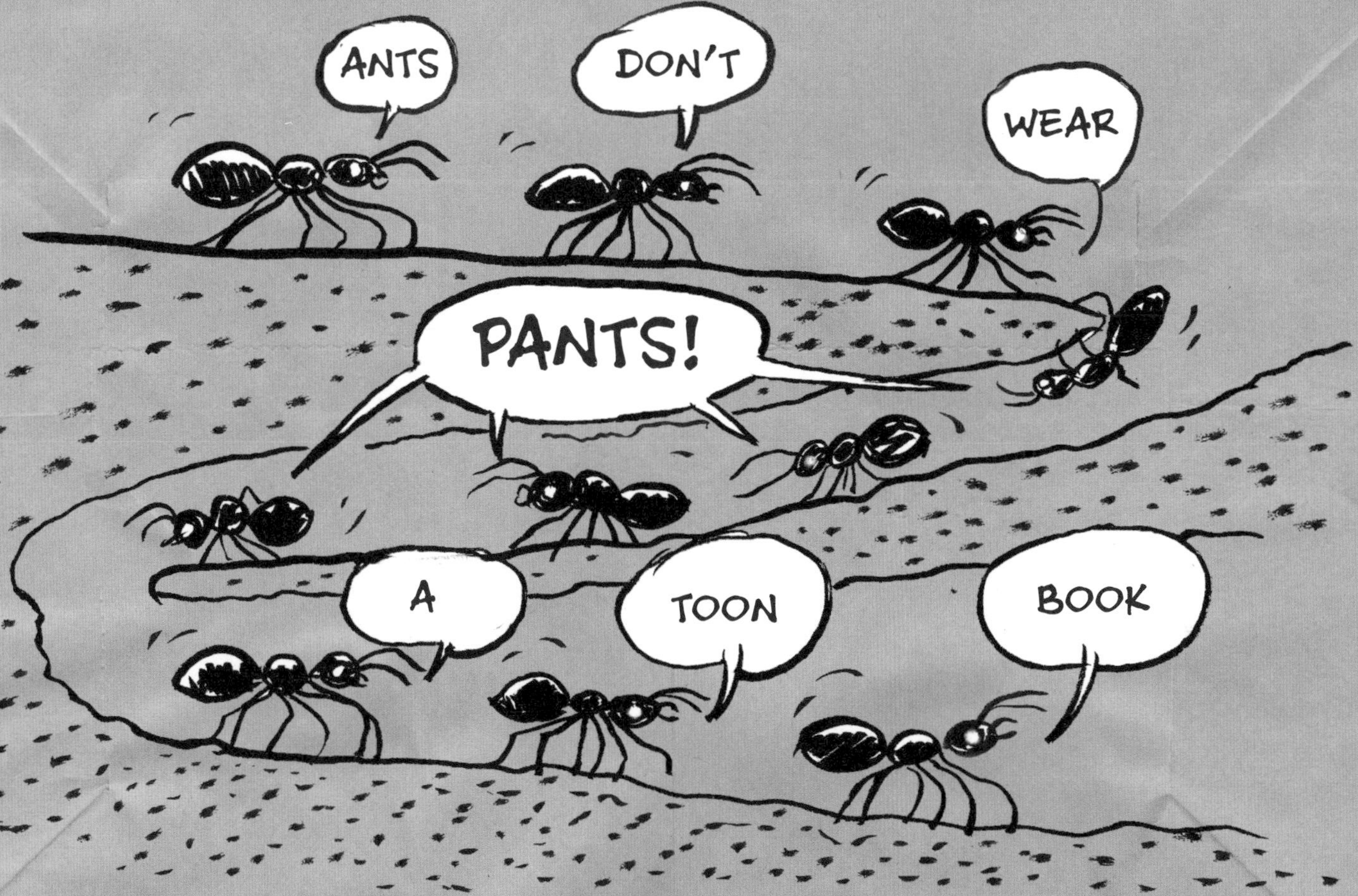
ANTS
DON'T
WEAR
PANTS!
A
TOON
BOOK

KEVIN McCLOSKEY

TOON BOOKS • NEW YORK

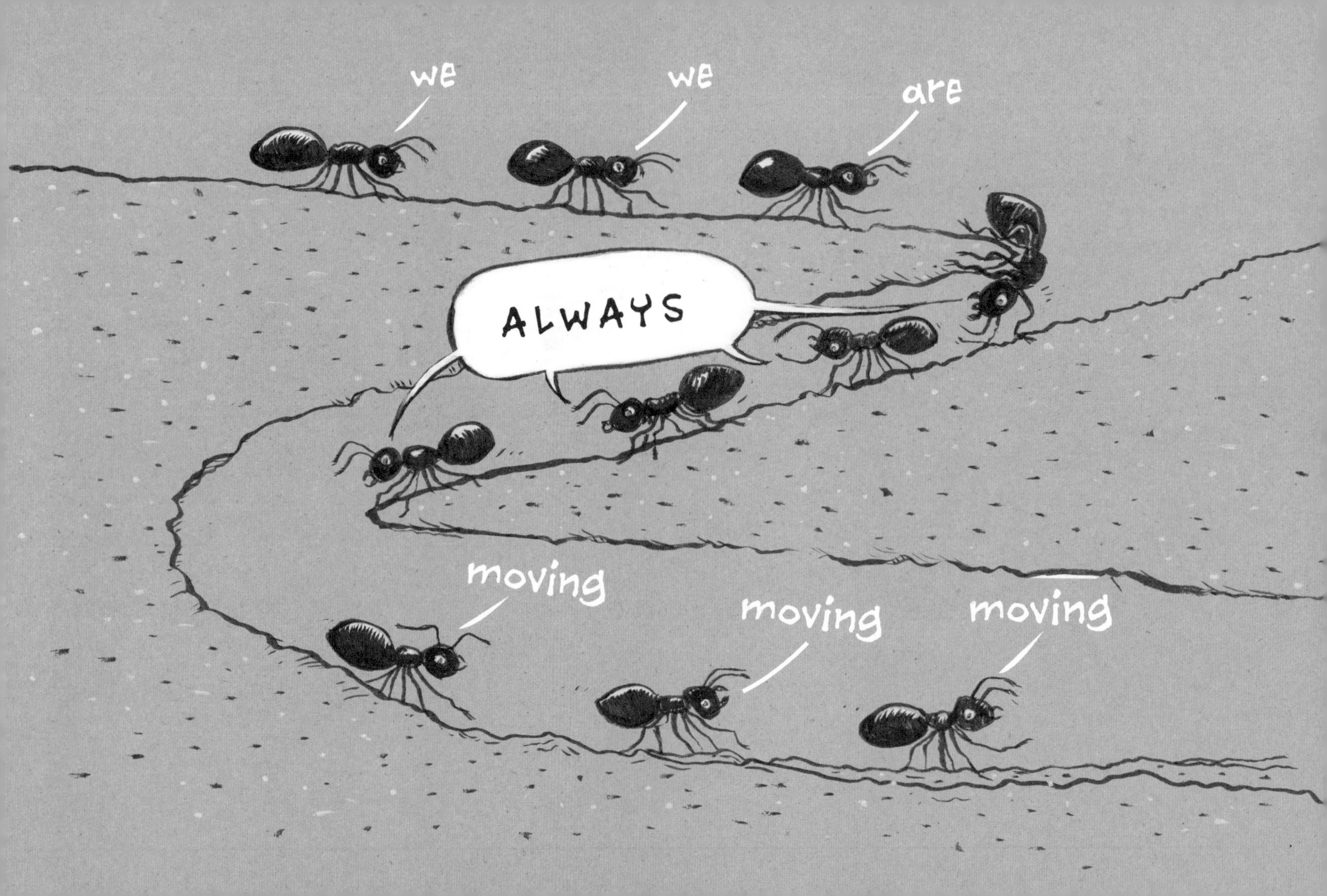
we
we
are
ALWAYS
moving
moving
moving

WHEN YOU CAN'T STOP MOVING,
WE SAY YOU HAVE "ANTS IN YOUR PANTS."

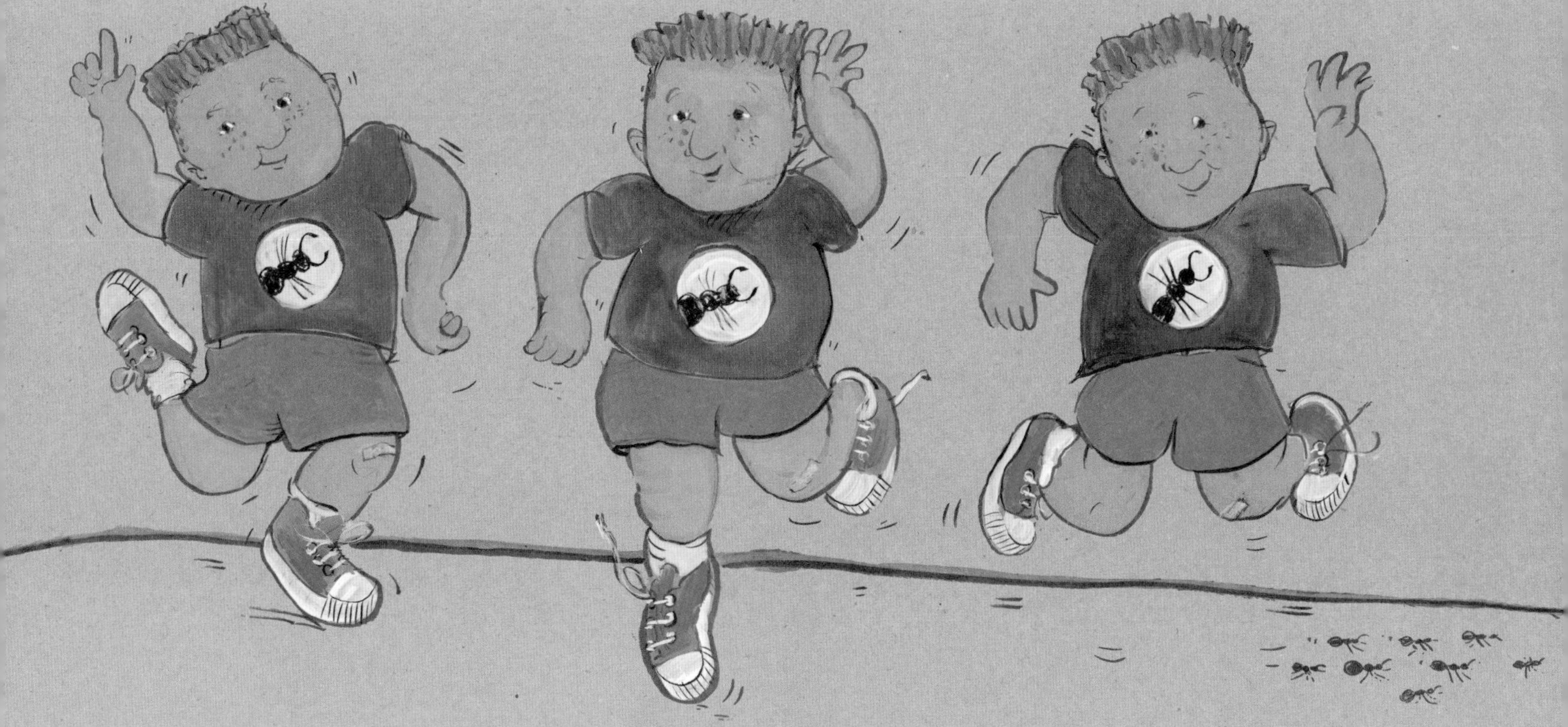

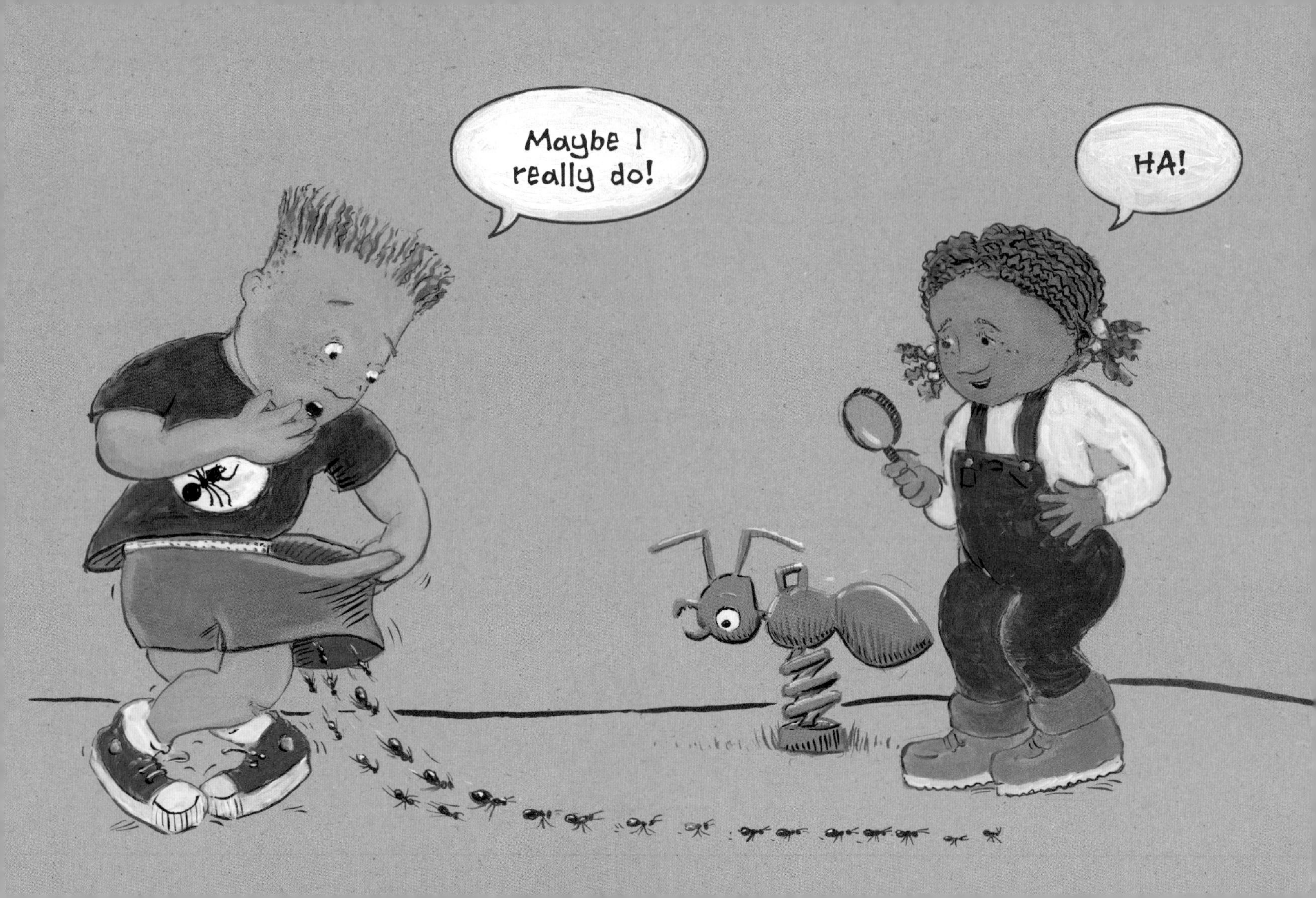
Maybe I really do!
HA!

ANTS ARE ALL AROUND US.
LOOK AND YOU WILL
FIND ANTHILLS.

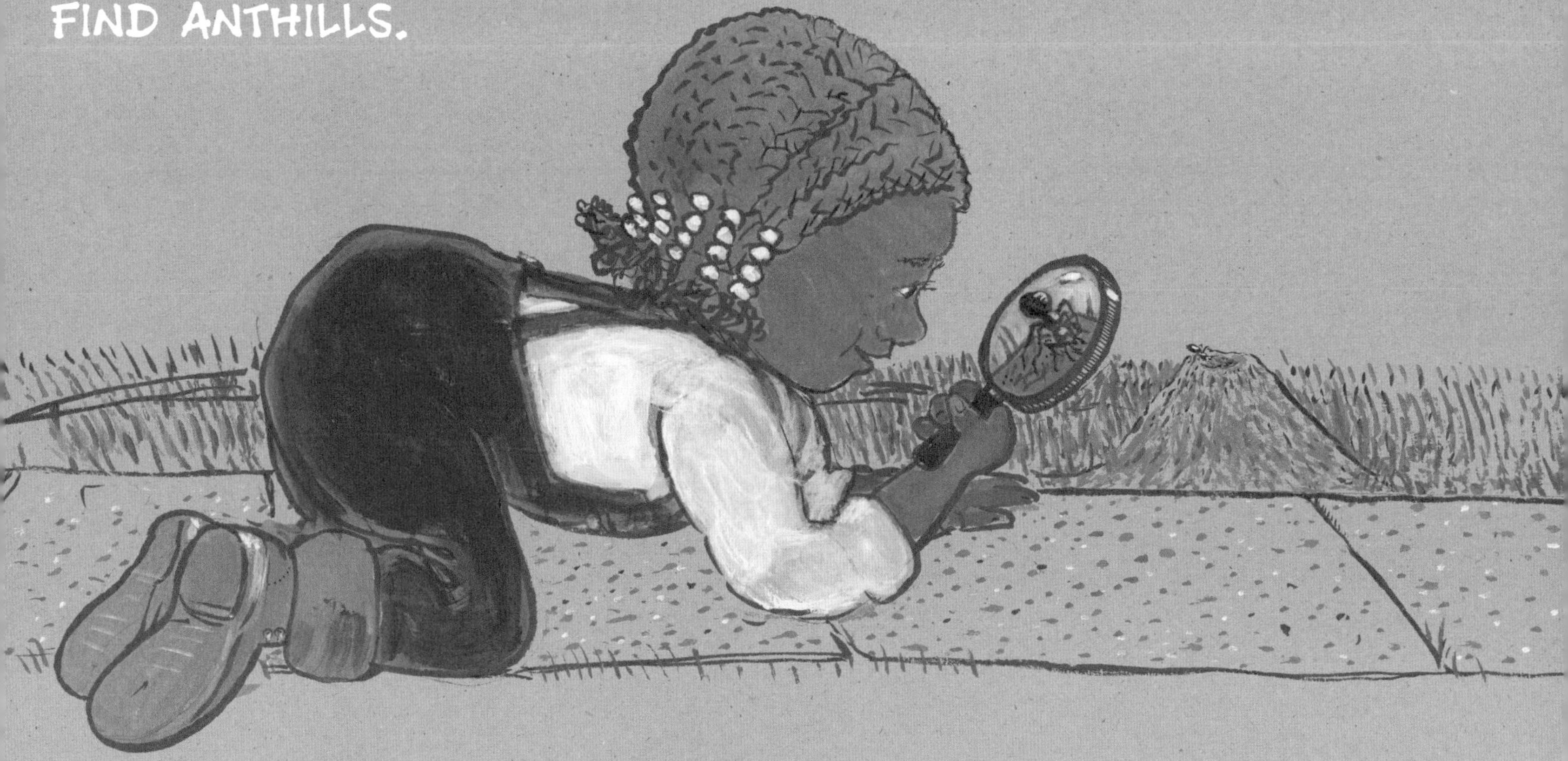

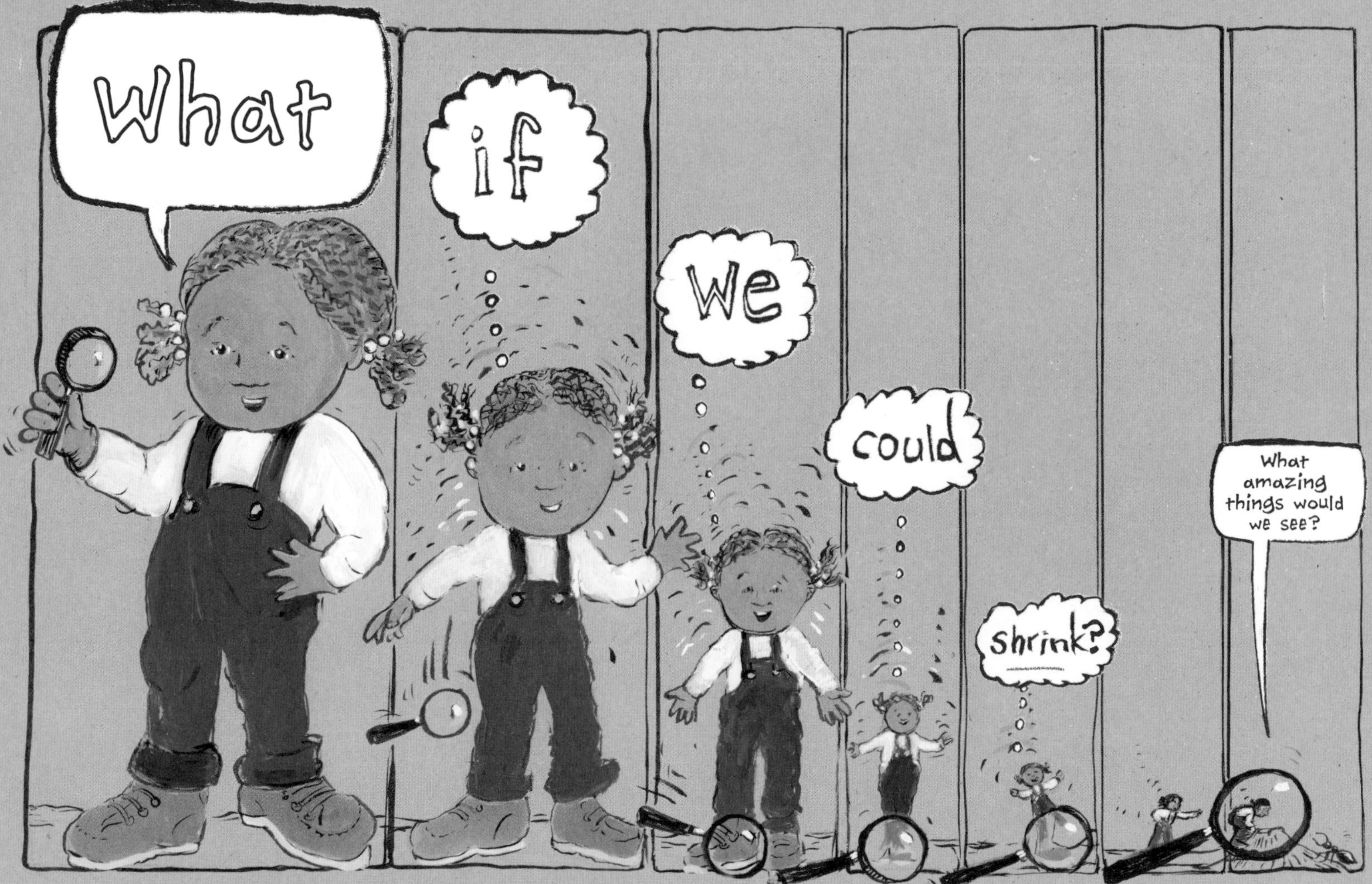
What
if
we
could
shrink?
What amazing things would we see?

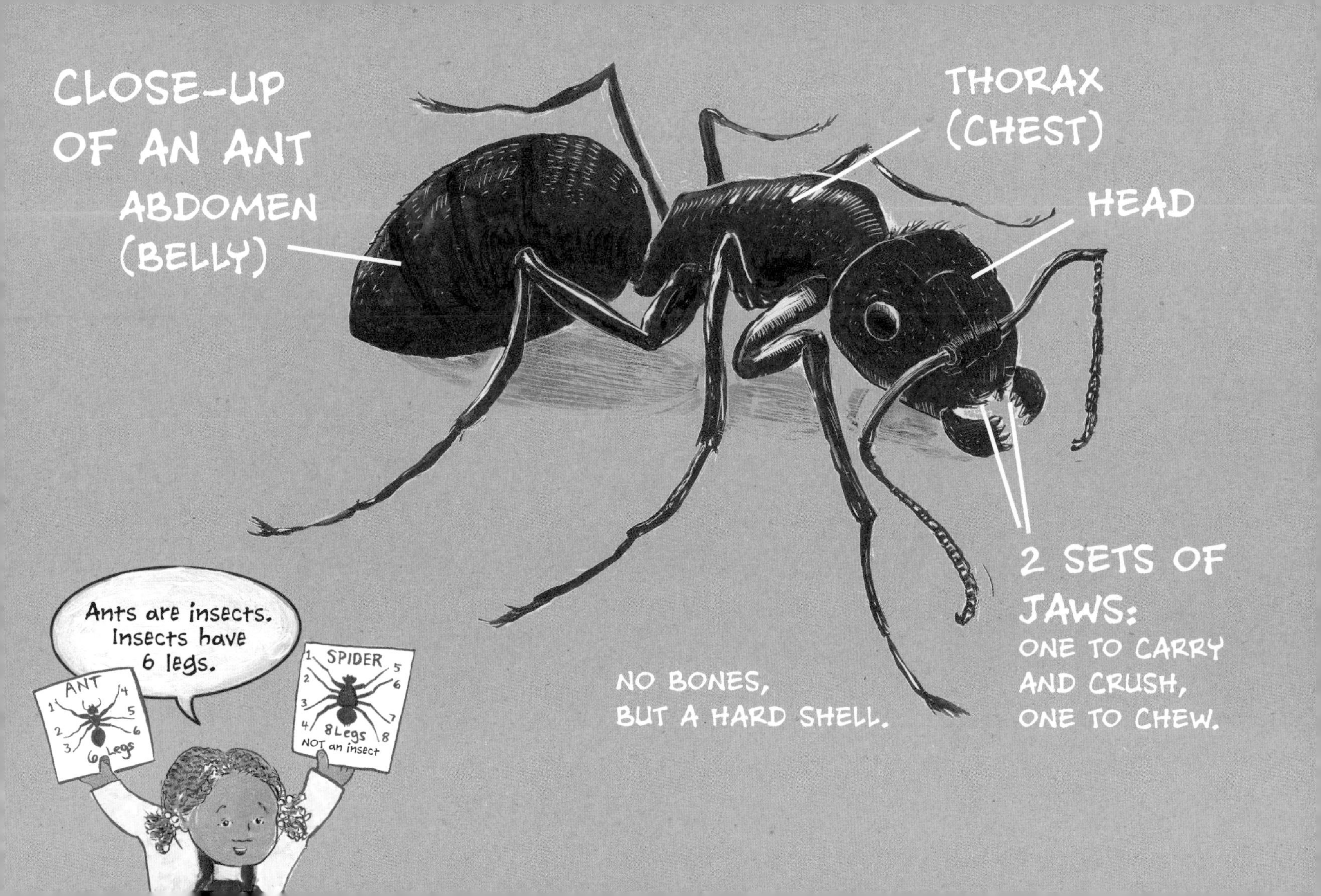
CLOSE-UP OF AN ANT
ABDOMEN (BELLY)
THORAX (CHEST)
HEAD
2 SETS OF JAWS:
ONE TO CARRY AND CRUSH, ONE TO CHEW.
NO BONES, BUT A HARD SHELL.
Ants are insects. Insects have 6 legs.
ANT
1 2 3 4 5 6 Legs
SPIDER
1 2 3 4 5 6 7 8 Legs
NOT an insect

ANTS HAVE TWO STOMACHS.
ONE IS JUST FOR SHARING.

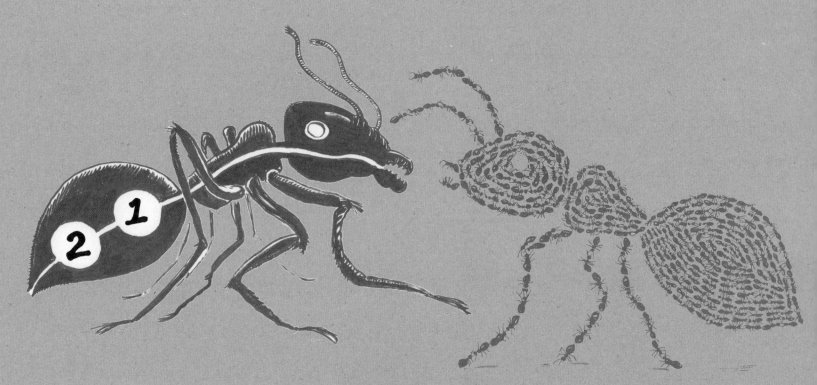

THEY SHARE FOOD WITH THE WHOLE COLONY.

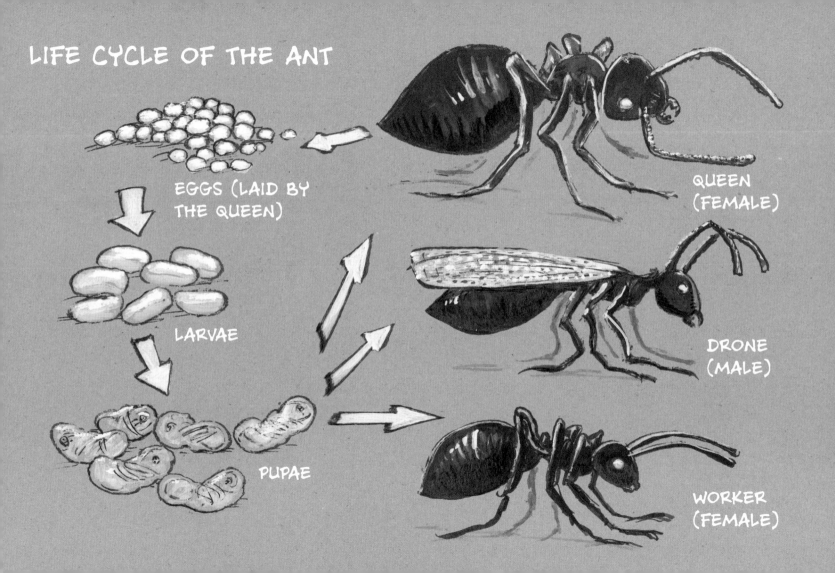

LIFE CYCLE OF THE ANT

EGGS (LAID BY THE QUEEN)

LARVAE

PUPAE

QUEEN (FEMALE)

DRONE (MALE)

WORKER (FEMALE)

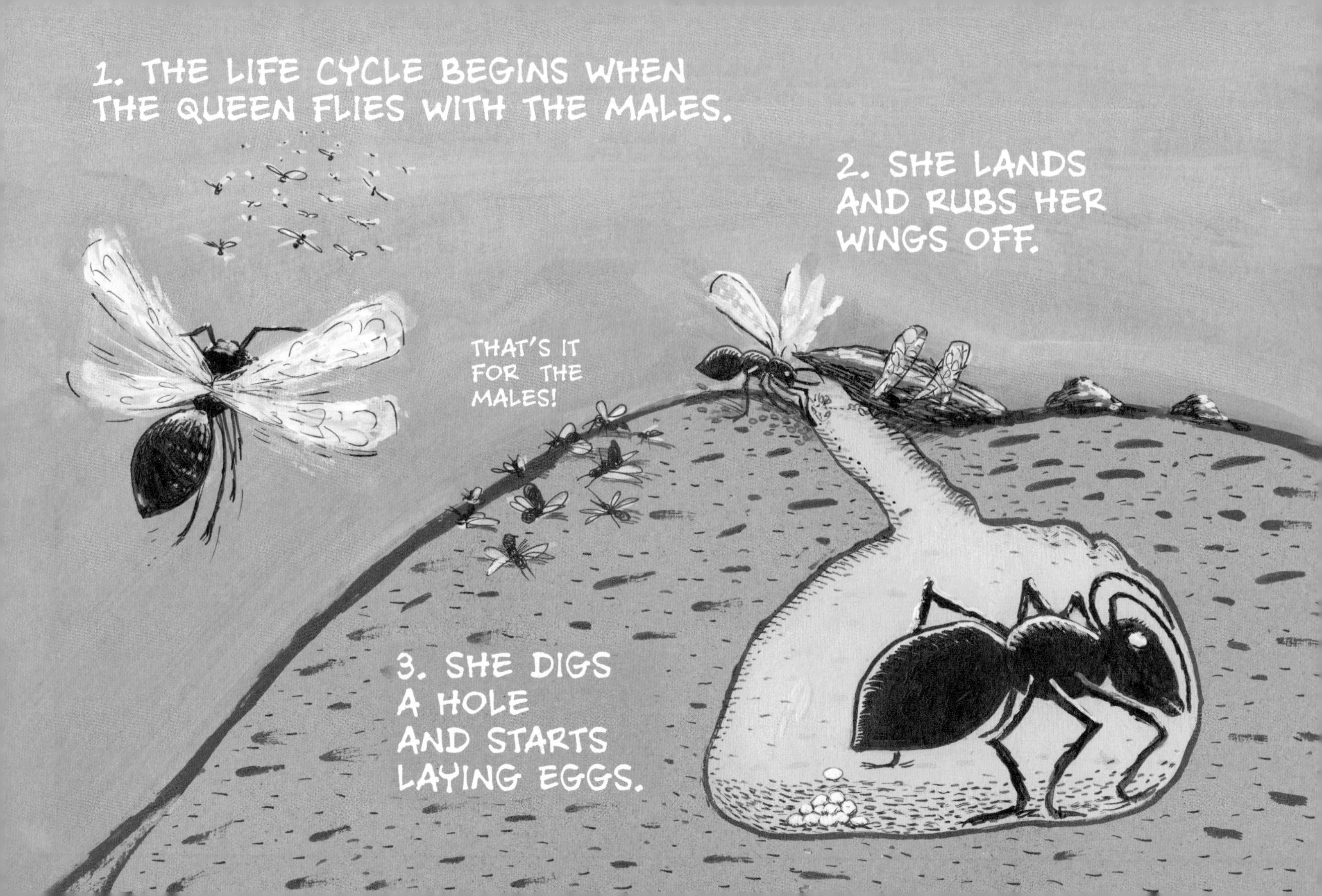
1. THE LIFE CYCLE BEGINS WHEN THE QUEEN FLIES WITH THE MALES.
2. SHE LANDS AND RUBS HER WINGS OFF.
THAT'S IT FOR THE MALES!
3. SHE DIGS A HOLE AND STARTS LAYING EGGS.

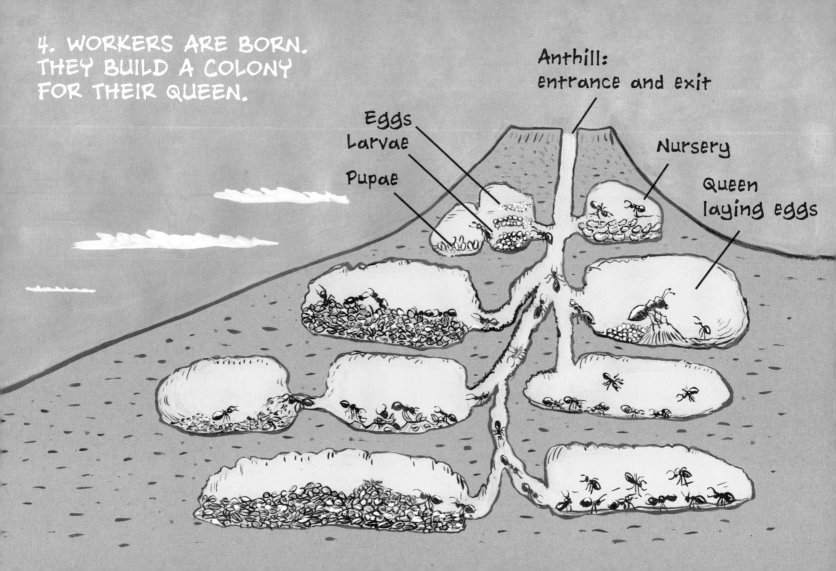

4. WORKERS ARE BORN. THEY BUILD A COLONY FOR THEIR QUEEN.

Eggs
Larvae
Pupae
Anthill: entrance and exit
Nursery
Queen laying eggs

ANTS DON'T SEE WELL, BUT THEY USE FOUR SENSES:

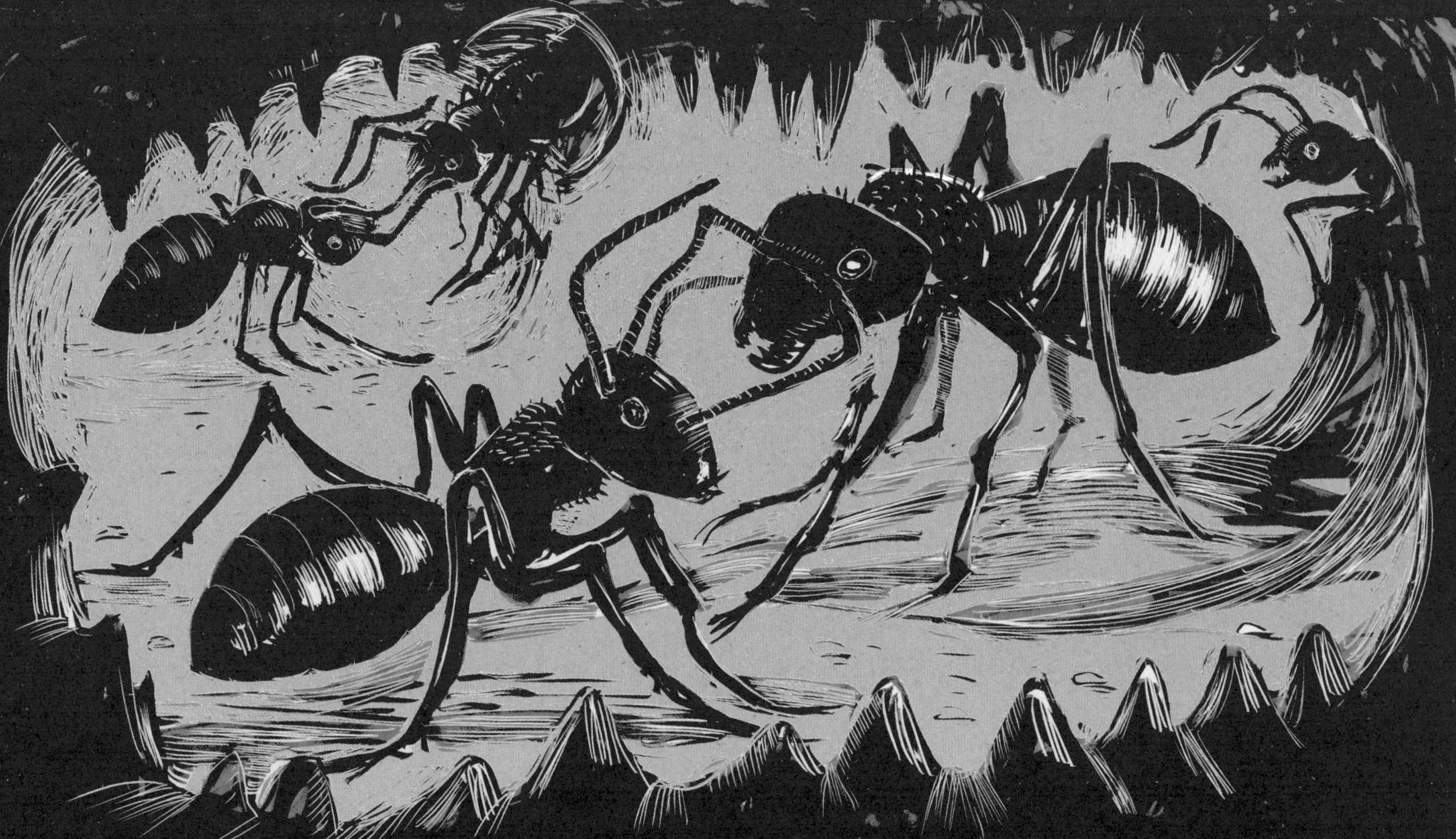

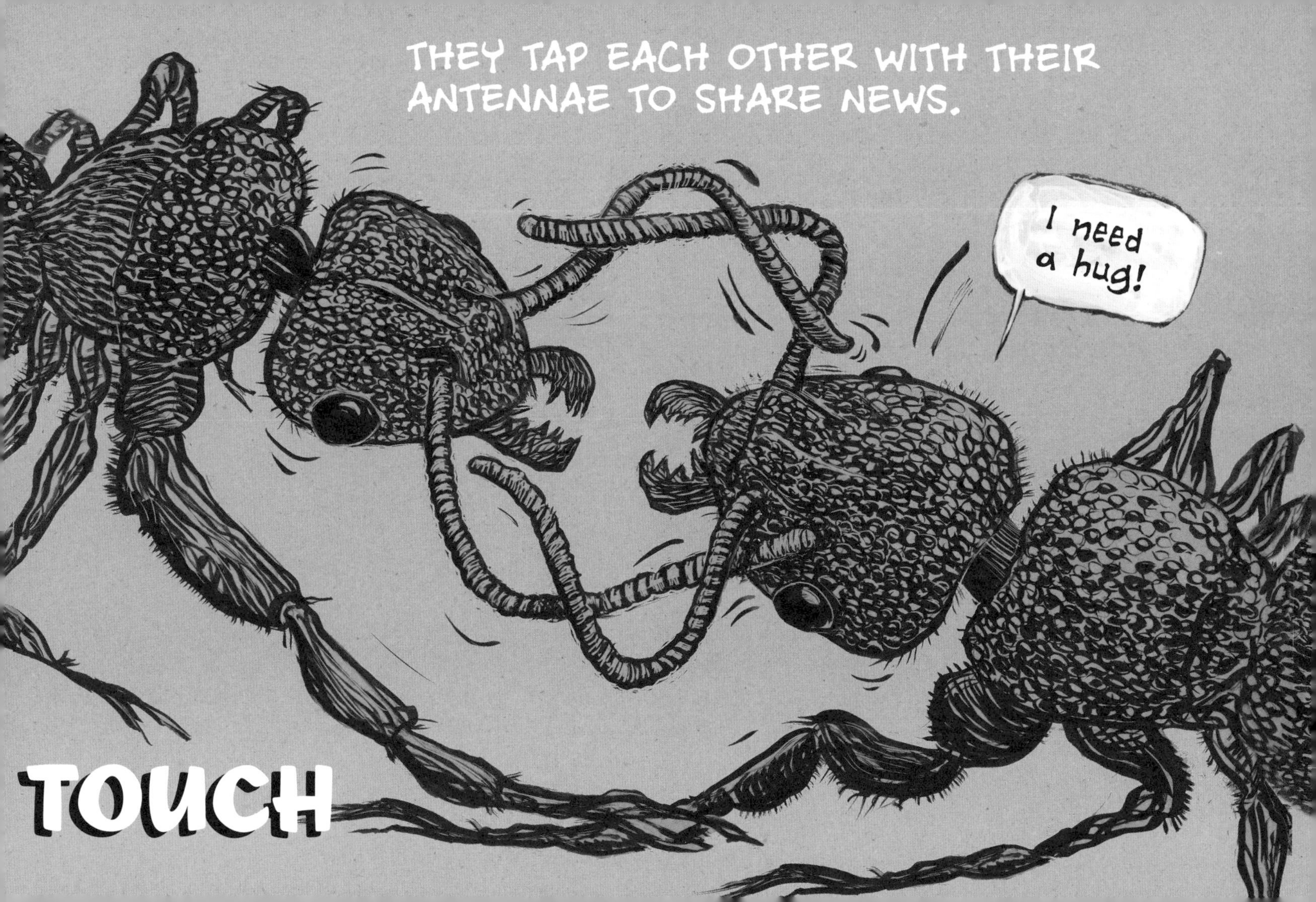
THEY TAP EACH OTHER WITH THEIR ANTENNAE TO SHARE NEWS.
I need a hug!
TOUCH

HEARING

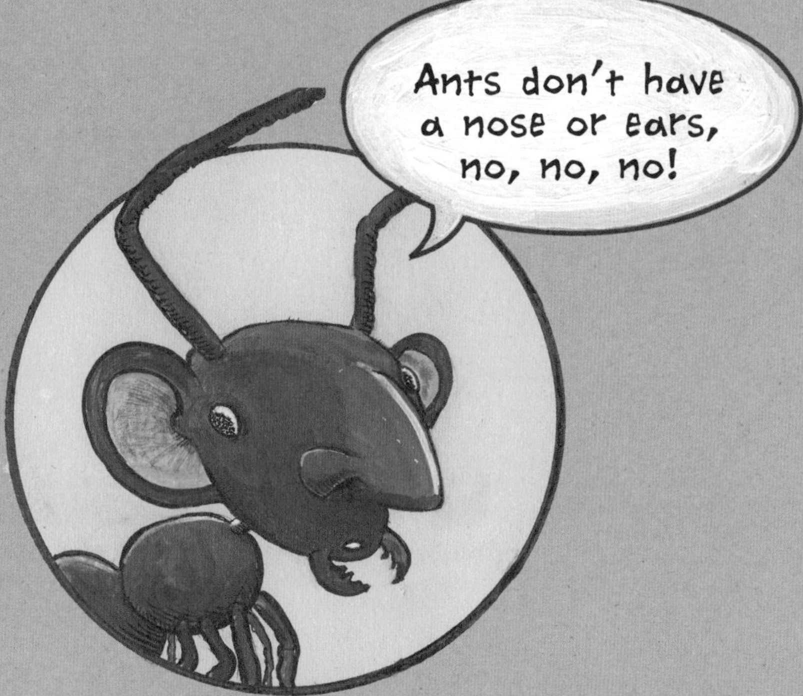
Ants don't have a nose or ears, no, no, no!

NO!

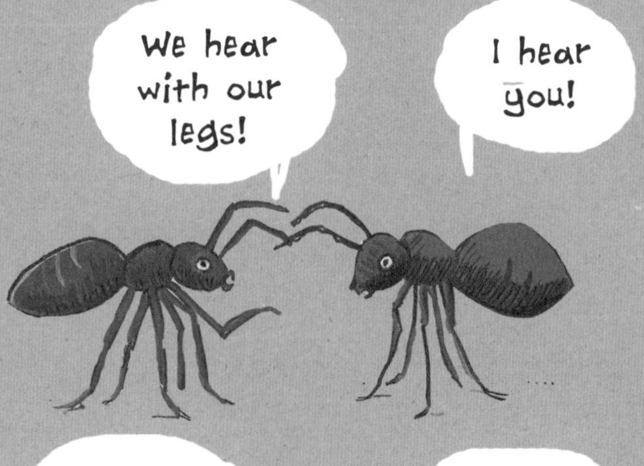
We hear with our legs!
I hear you!

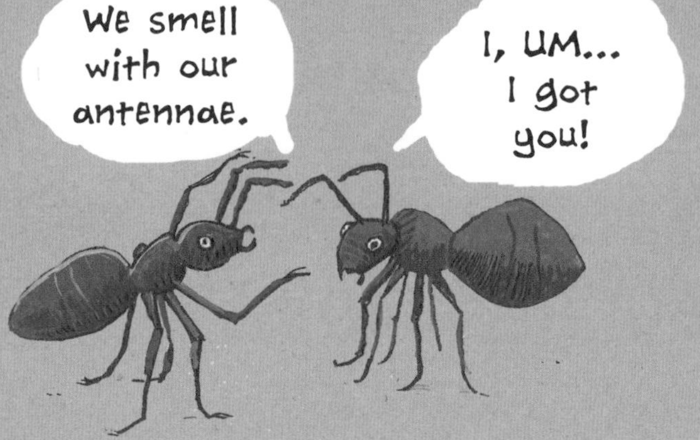
We smell with our antennae.
I, UM... I got you!

Ants feel, hug and smell with their antennae.

SMELL

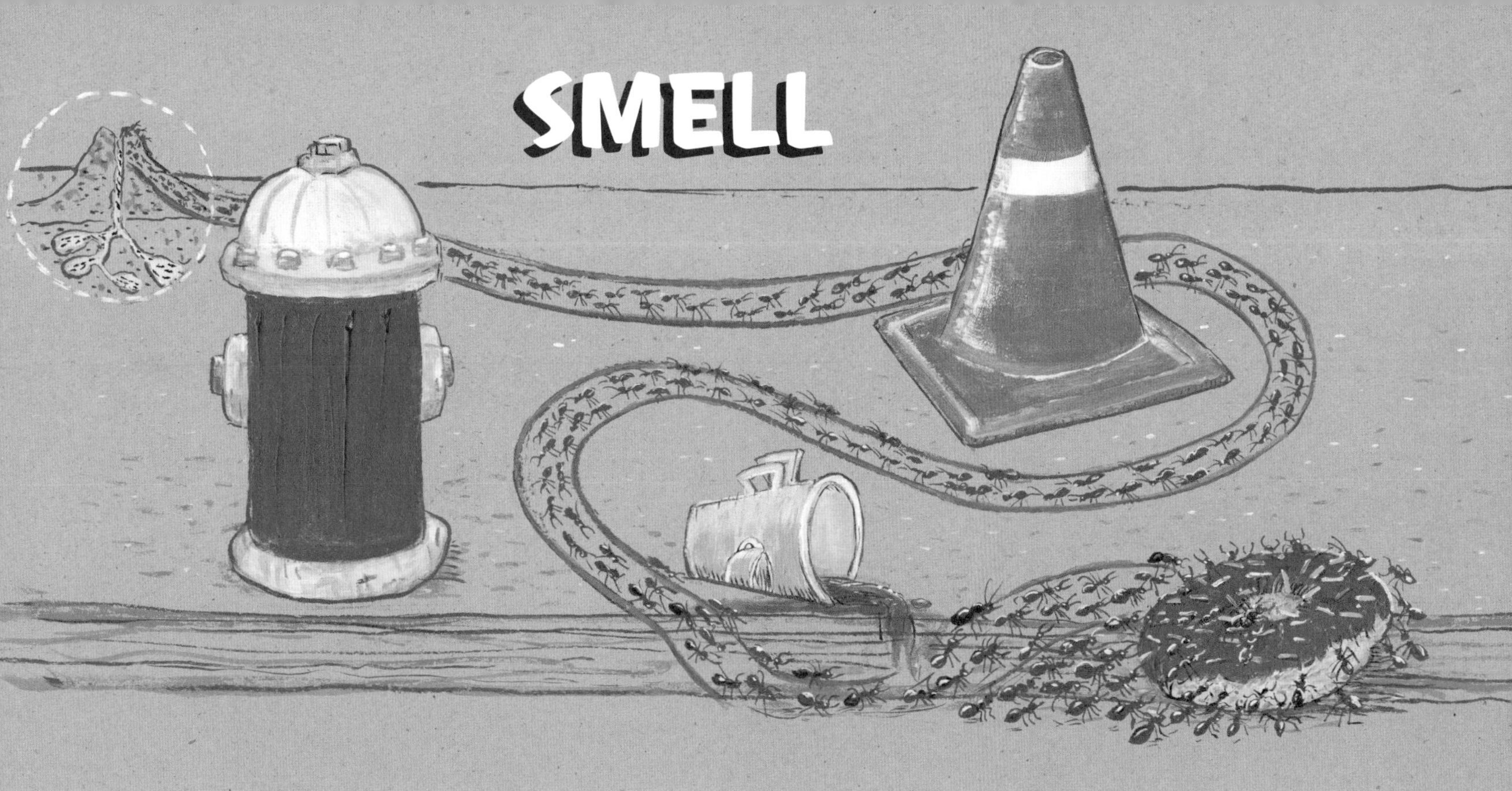

Scout ants bump their bottom to leave a smell trail back to food ( ).

TASTE

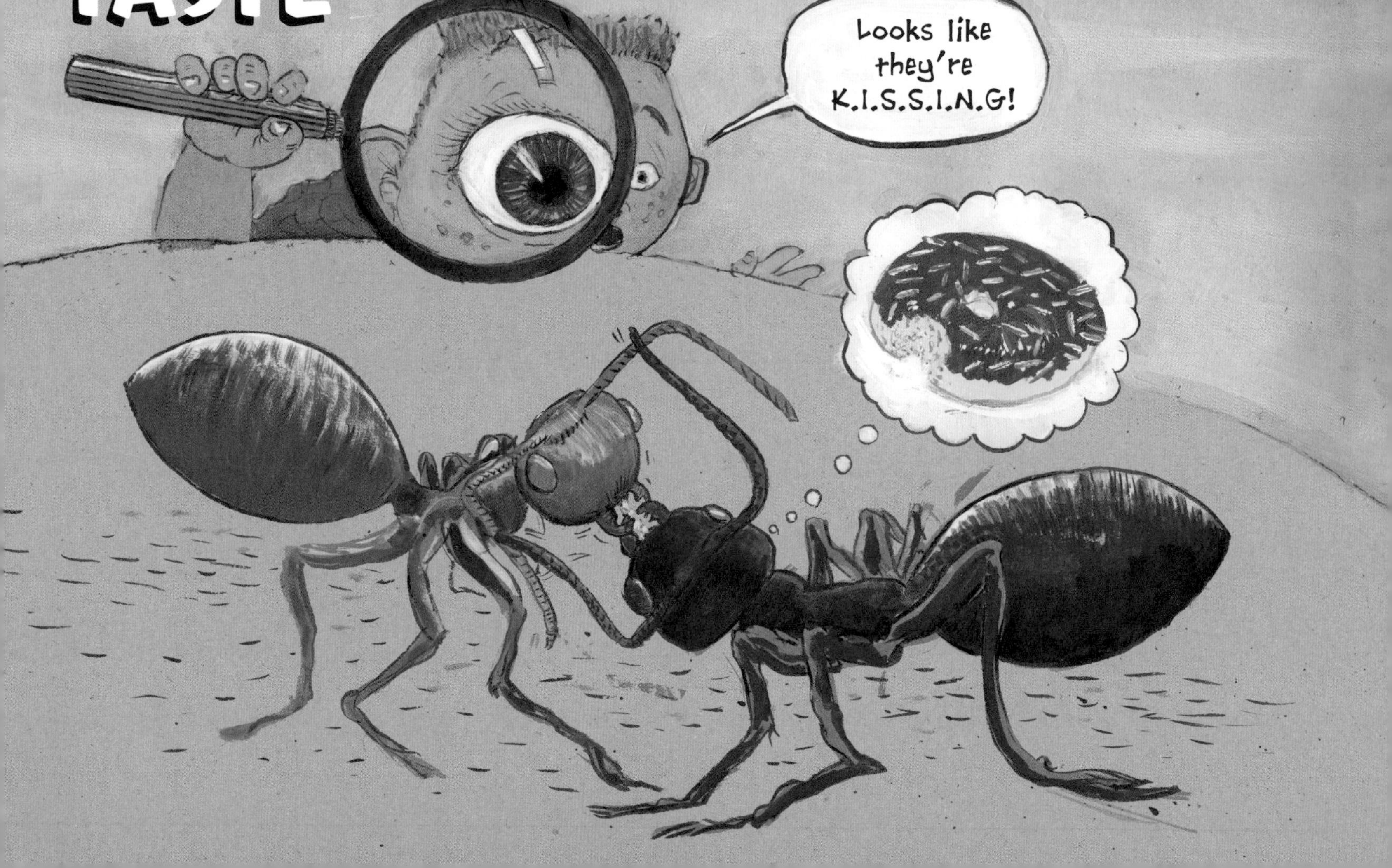
Looks like they're K.I.S.S.I.N.G!

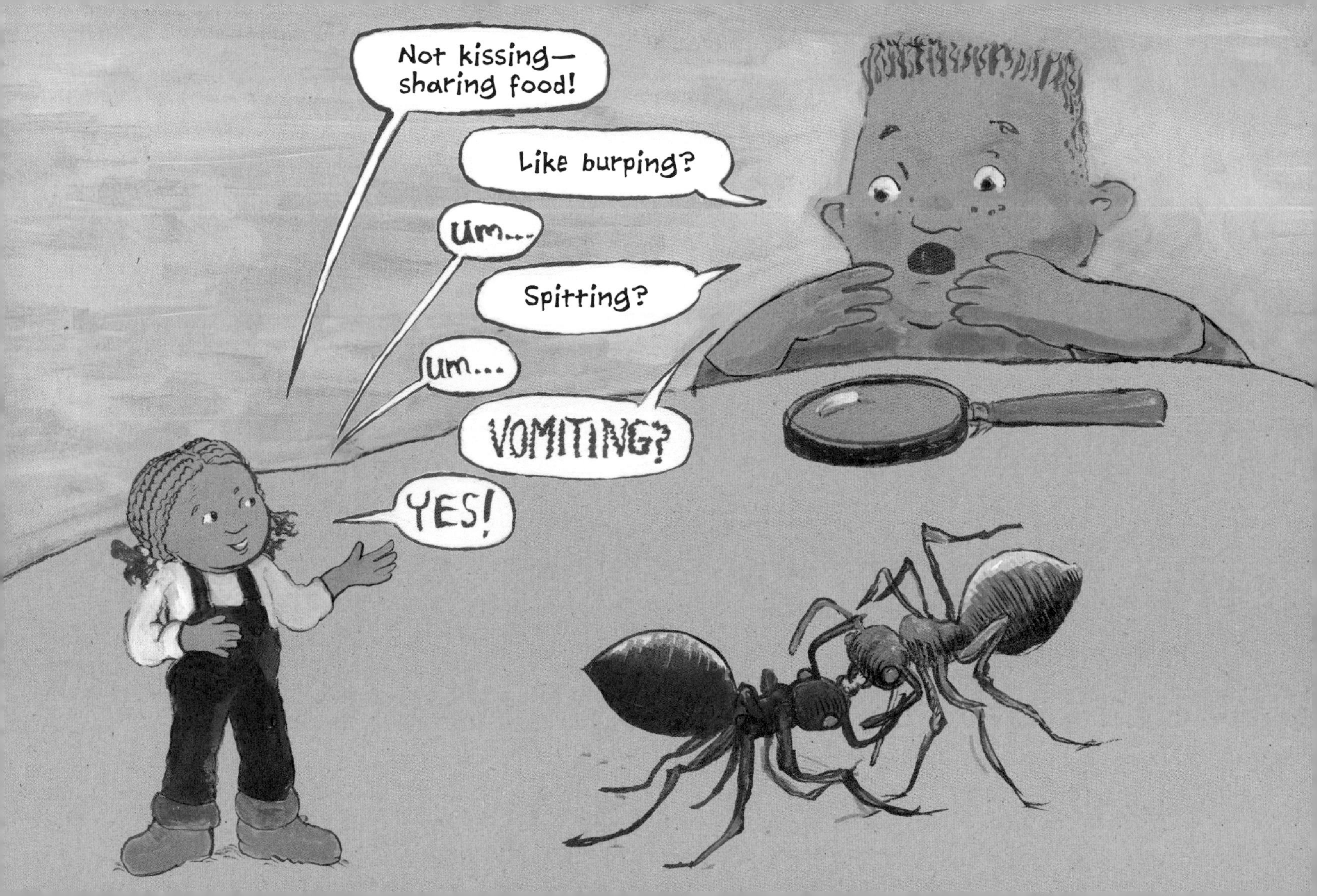

Not kissing—
sharing food!
Like burping?
Um...
Spitting?
um...
VOMITING?
YES!

THIS IS 1000 ANTS. SOME COLONIES ARE MUCH BIGGER.

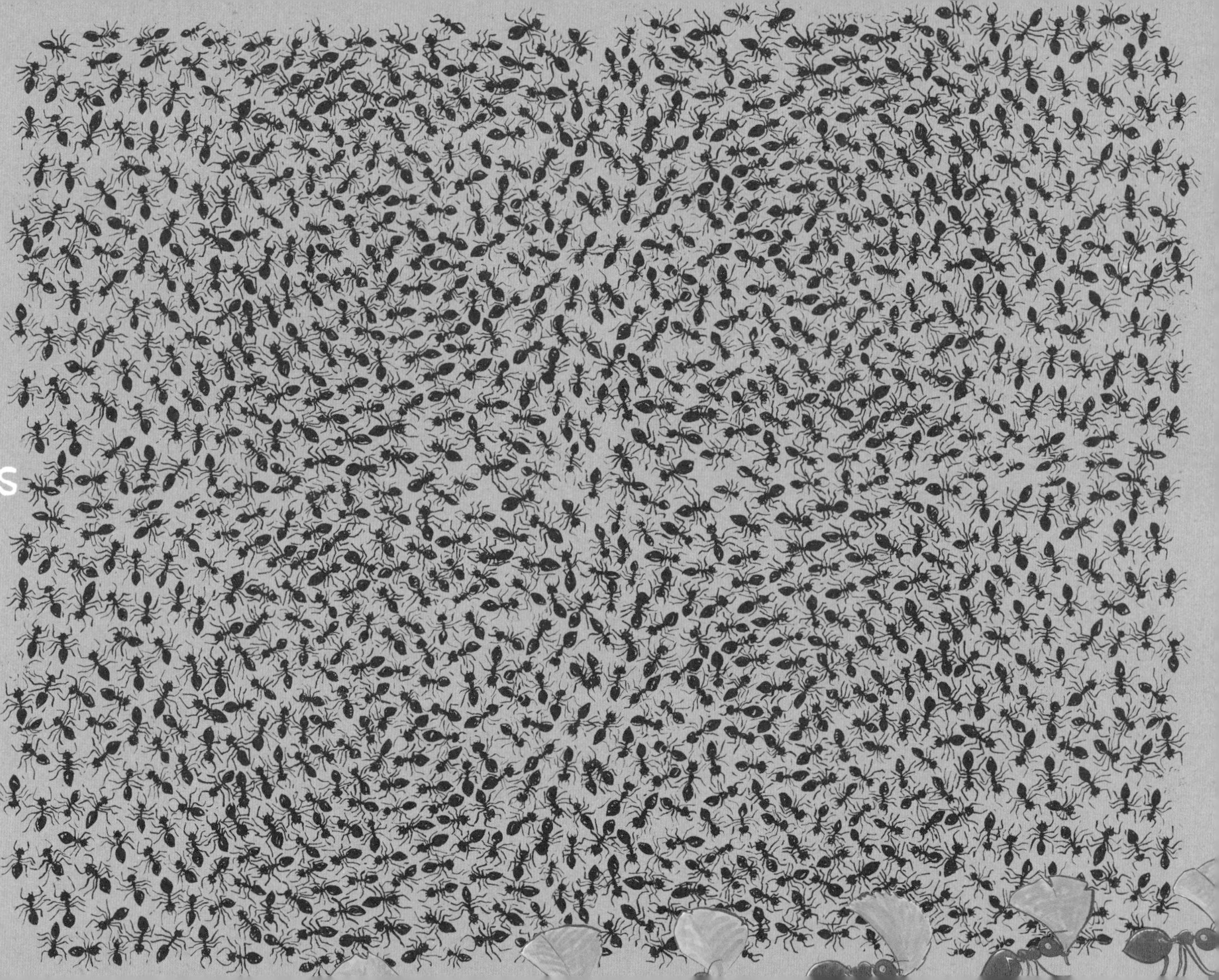

AND THERE ARE THOUSANDS OF KINDS OF ANTS:

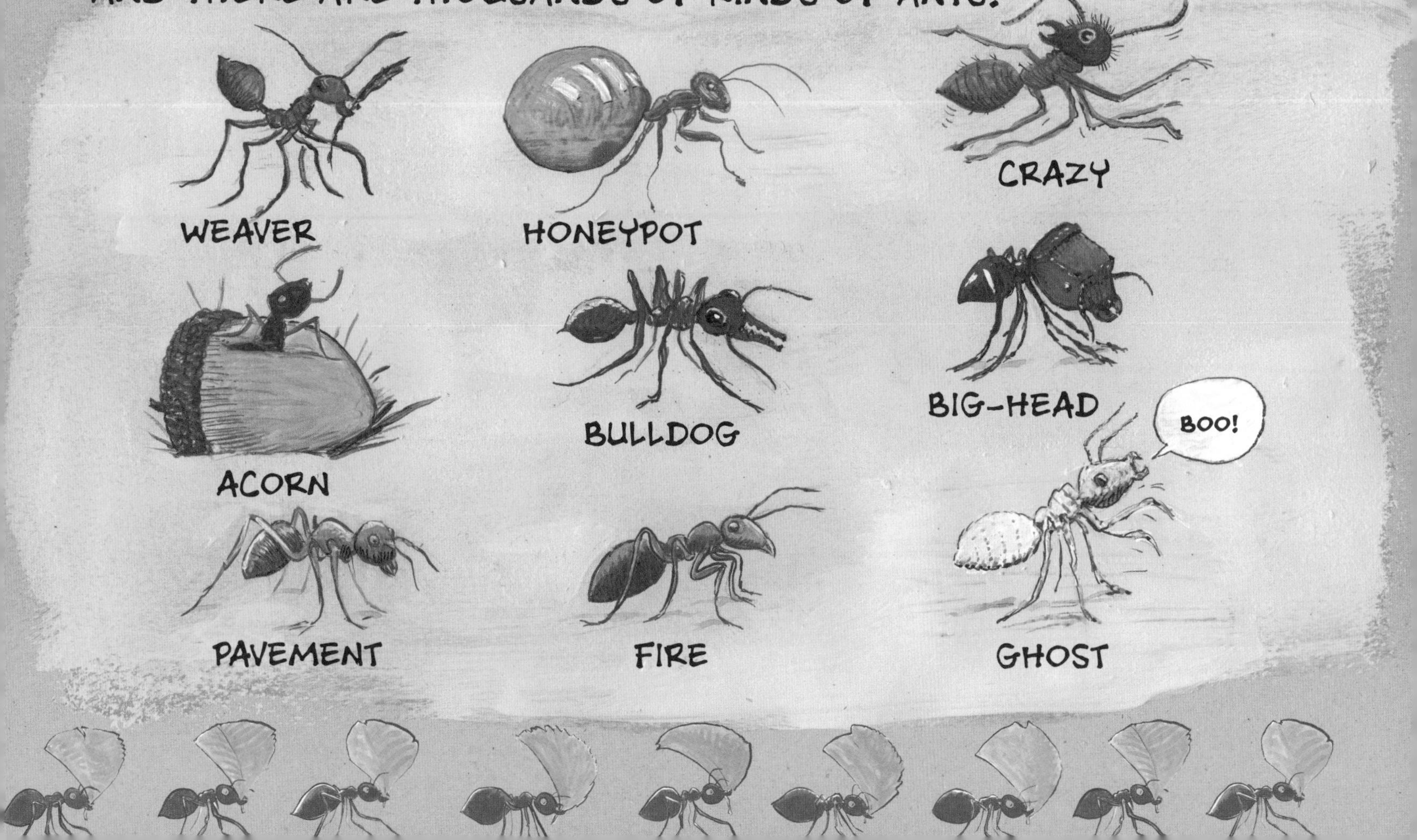
WEAVER
HONEYPOT
CRAZY
ACORN
BULLDOG
BIG-HEAD
BOO!
PAVEMENT
FIRE
GHOST

LEAF-CUTTER ANTS WORK TOGETHER TO FARM.

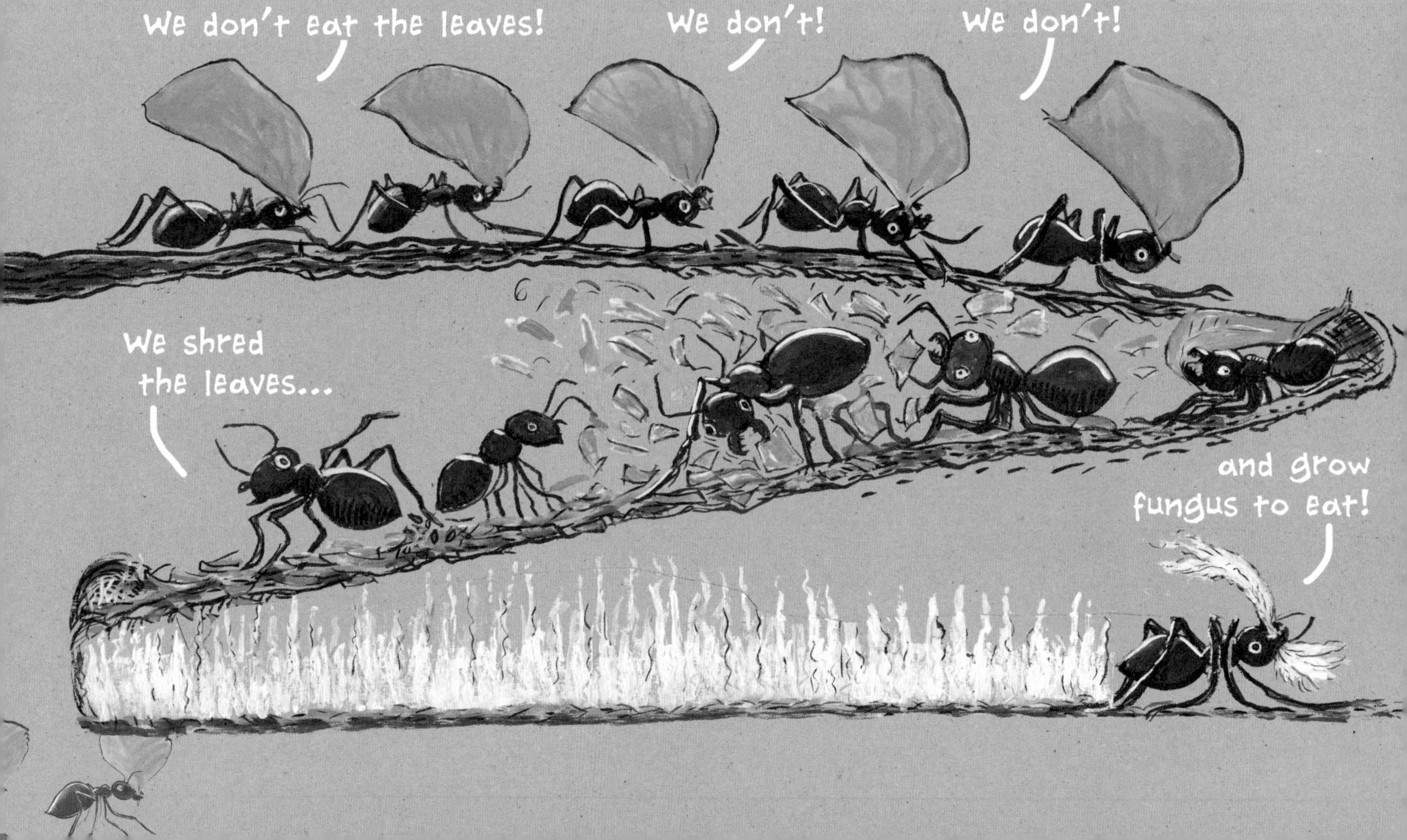
We don't eat the leaves!
We don't!
We don't!
We shred the leaves...
and grow fungus to eat!

SOME ANTS RAISE AND MILK TINY INSECTS.

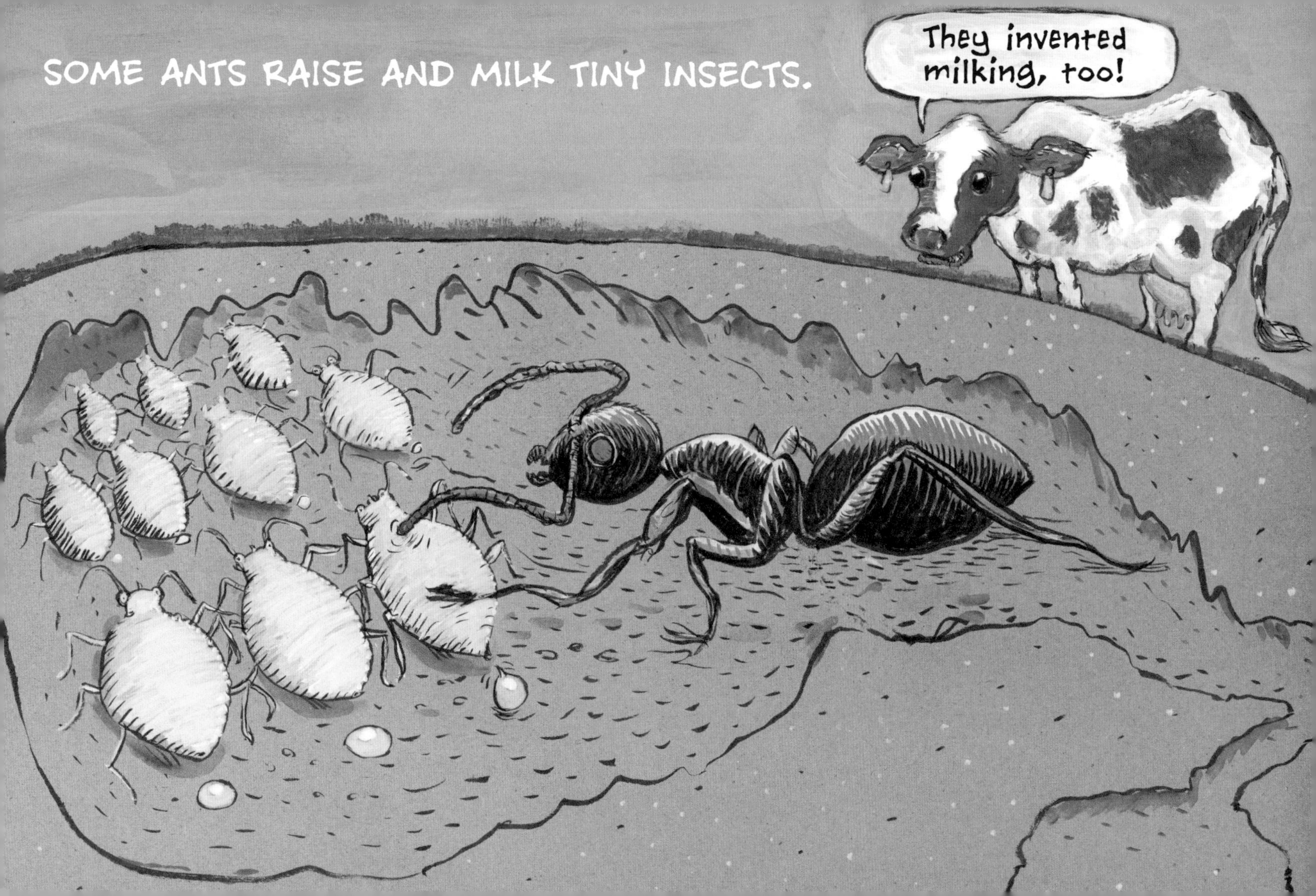
They invented milking, too!

A TRAP-JAW ANT CLOSES
ITS JAWS VERY, VERY FAST.

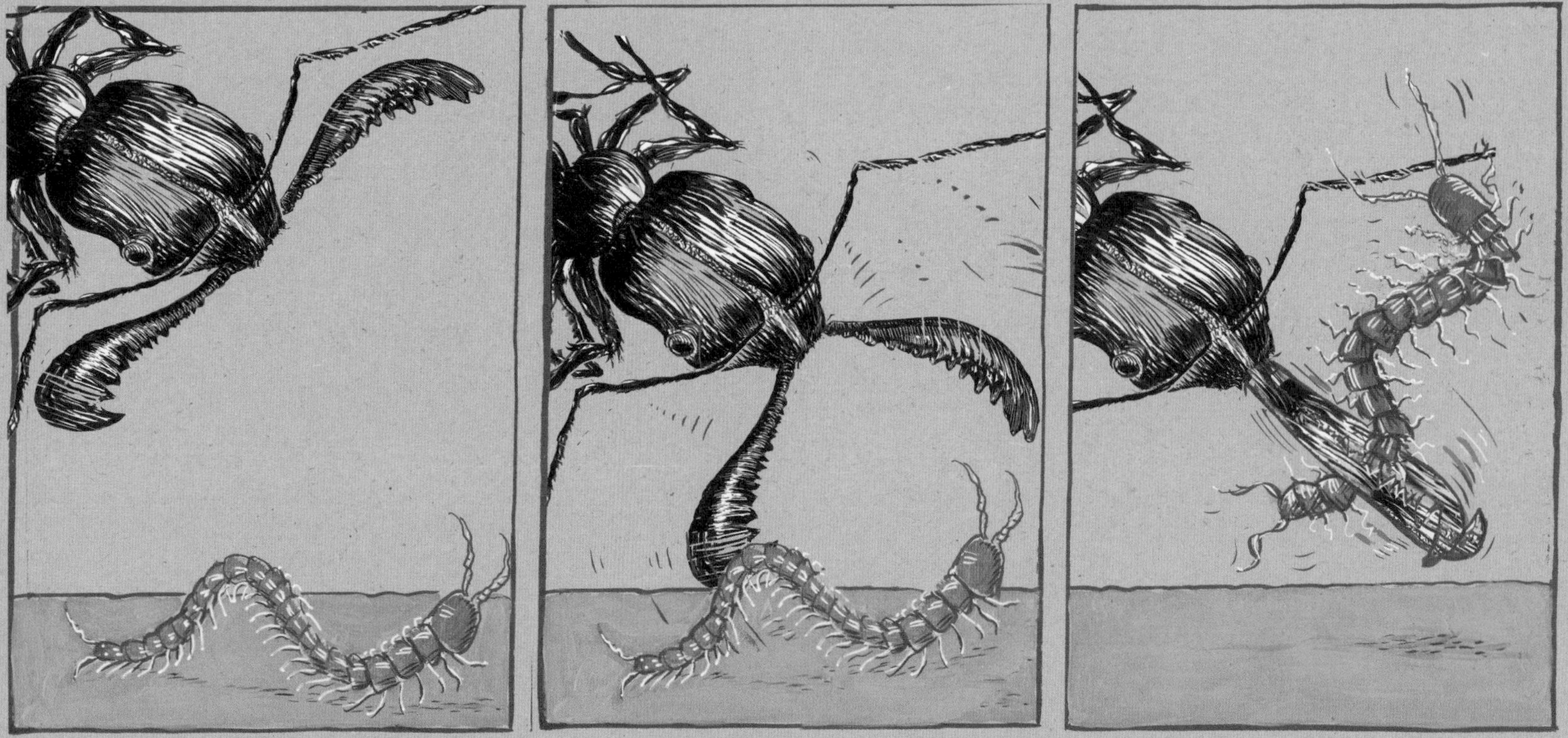

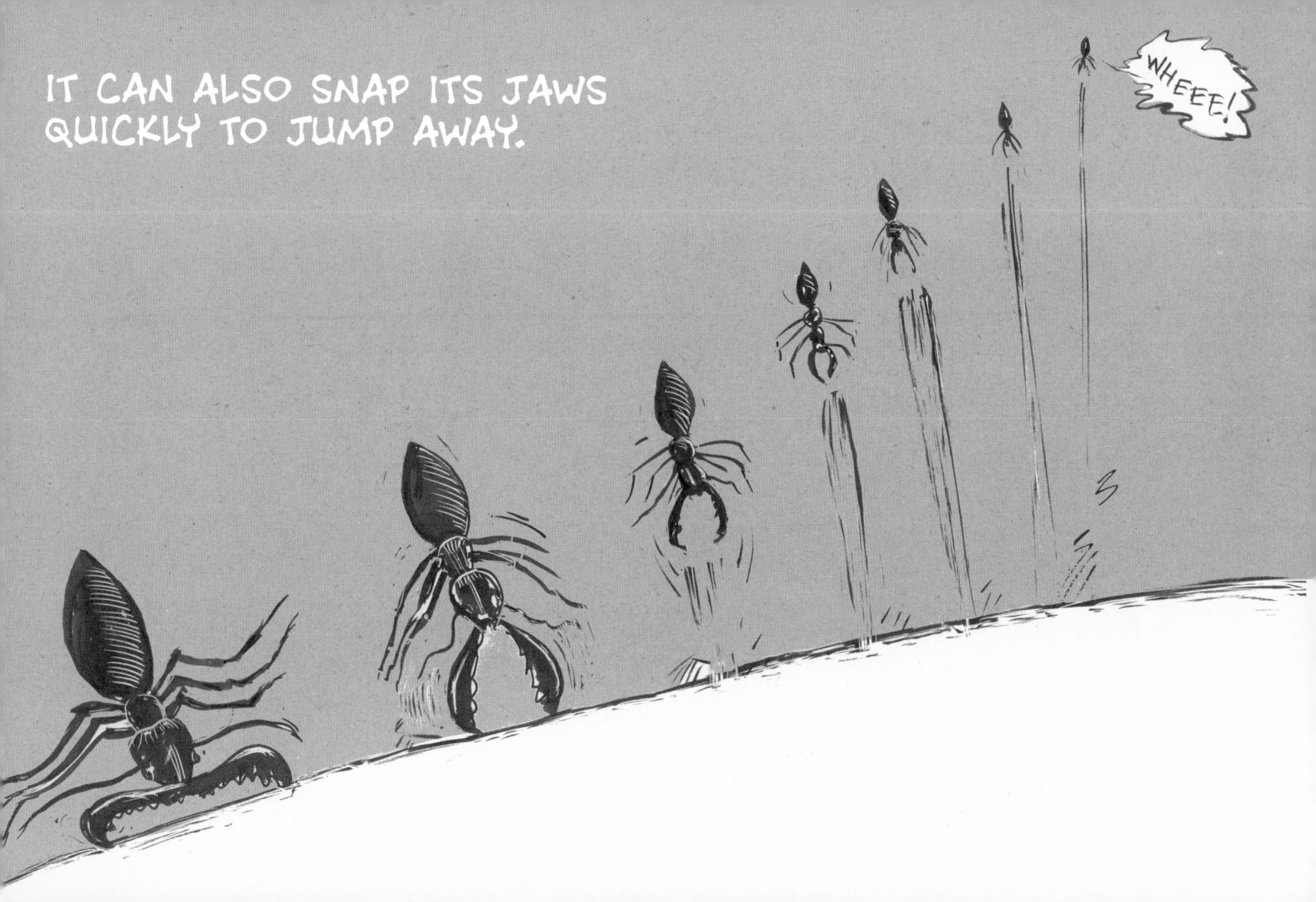
IT CAN ALSO SNAP ITS JAWS QUICKLY TO JUMP AWAY.
WHEEEE!

ANTS CAN LIFT UP TO 50 TIMES THEIR OWN WEIGHT.

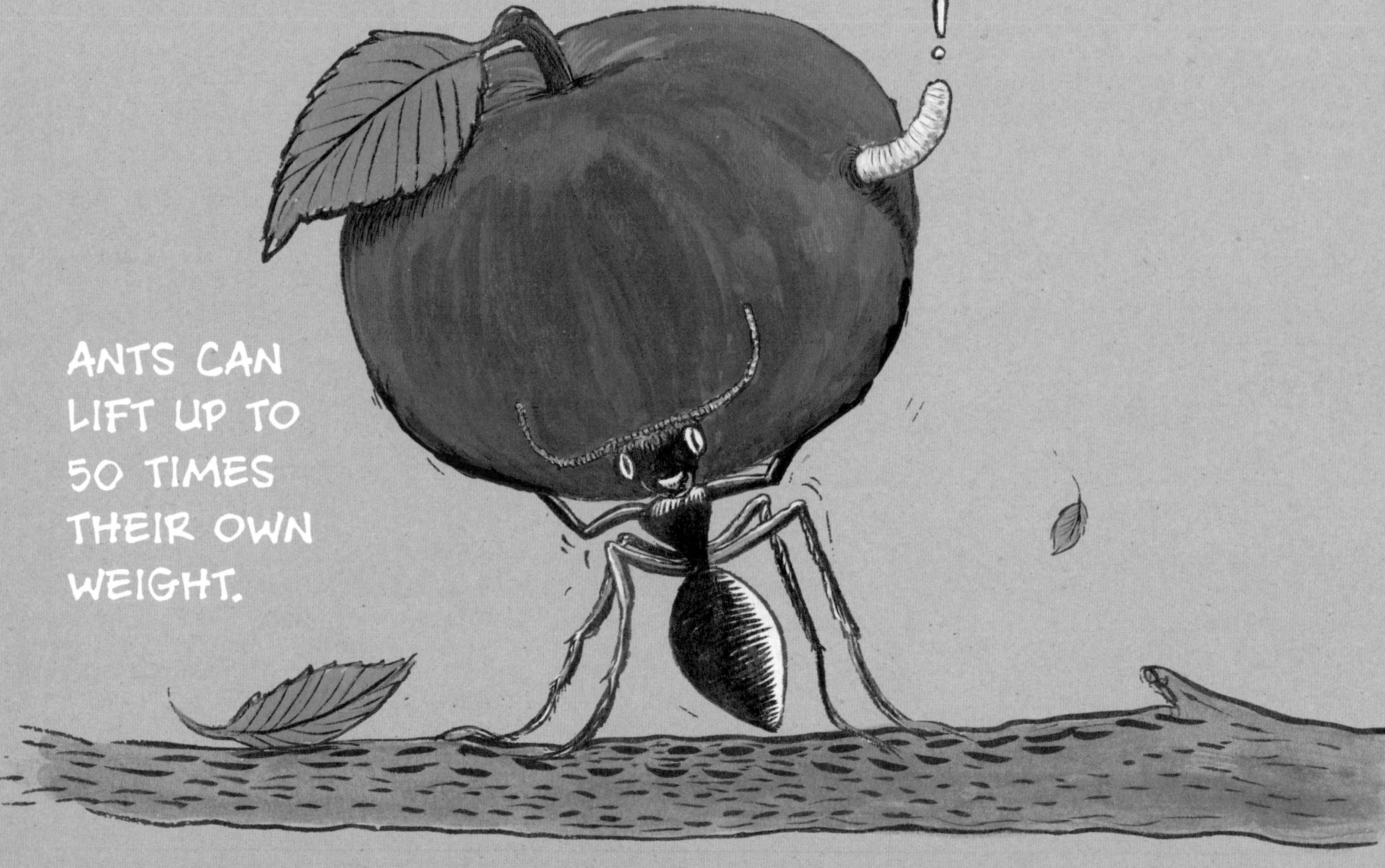
!

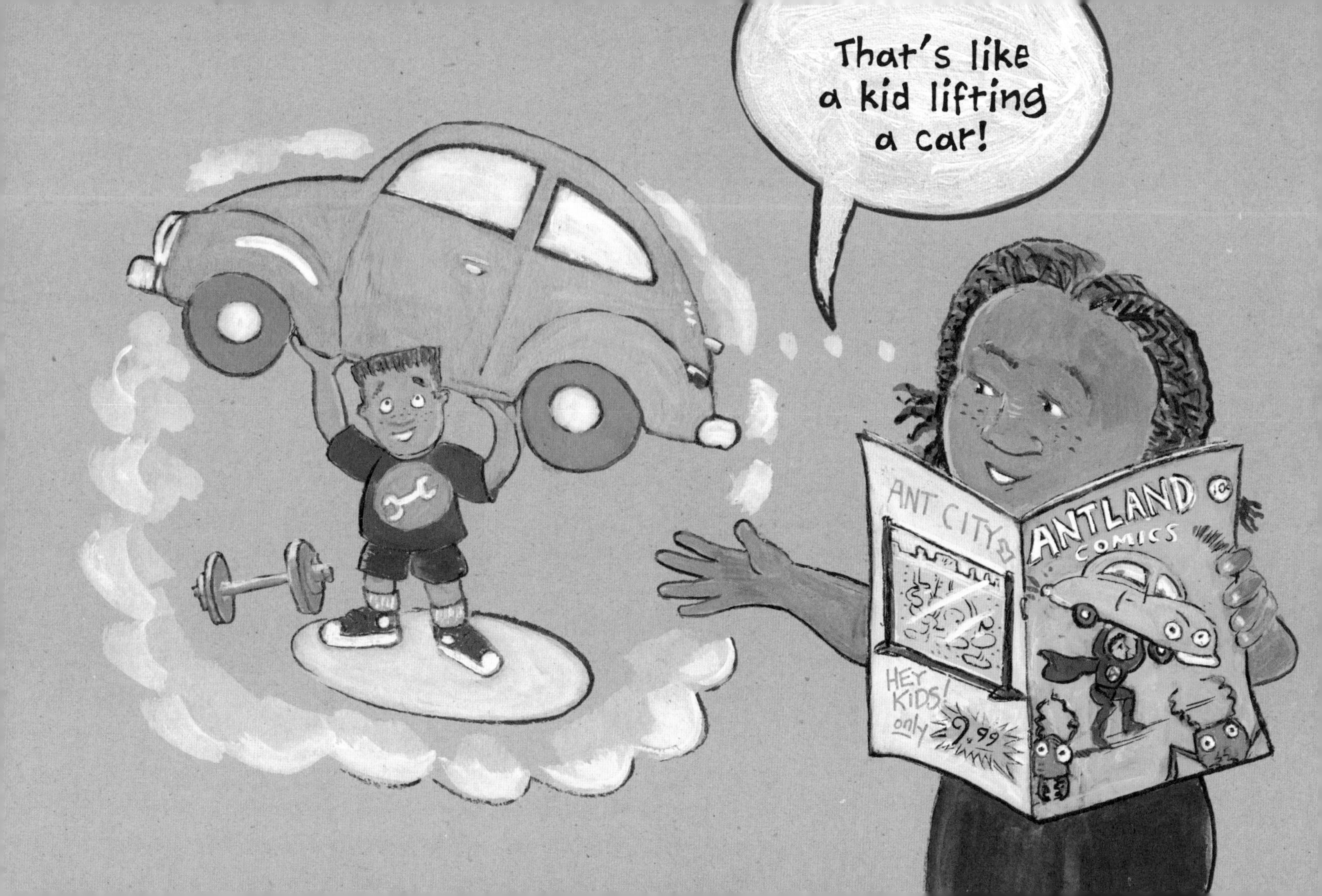
That's like a kid lifting a car!
ANT CITY
ANTLAND COMICS
10¢
HEY KIDS! only 9.99

SOME ANTS LIVE IN TREES. ELEPHANTS ARE SCARED OF THEM.

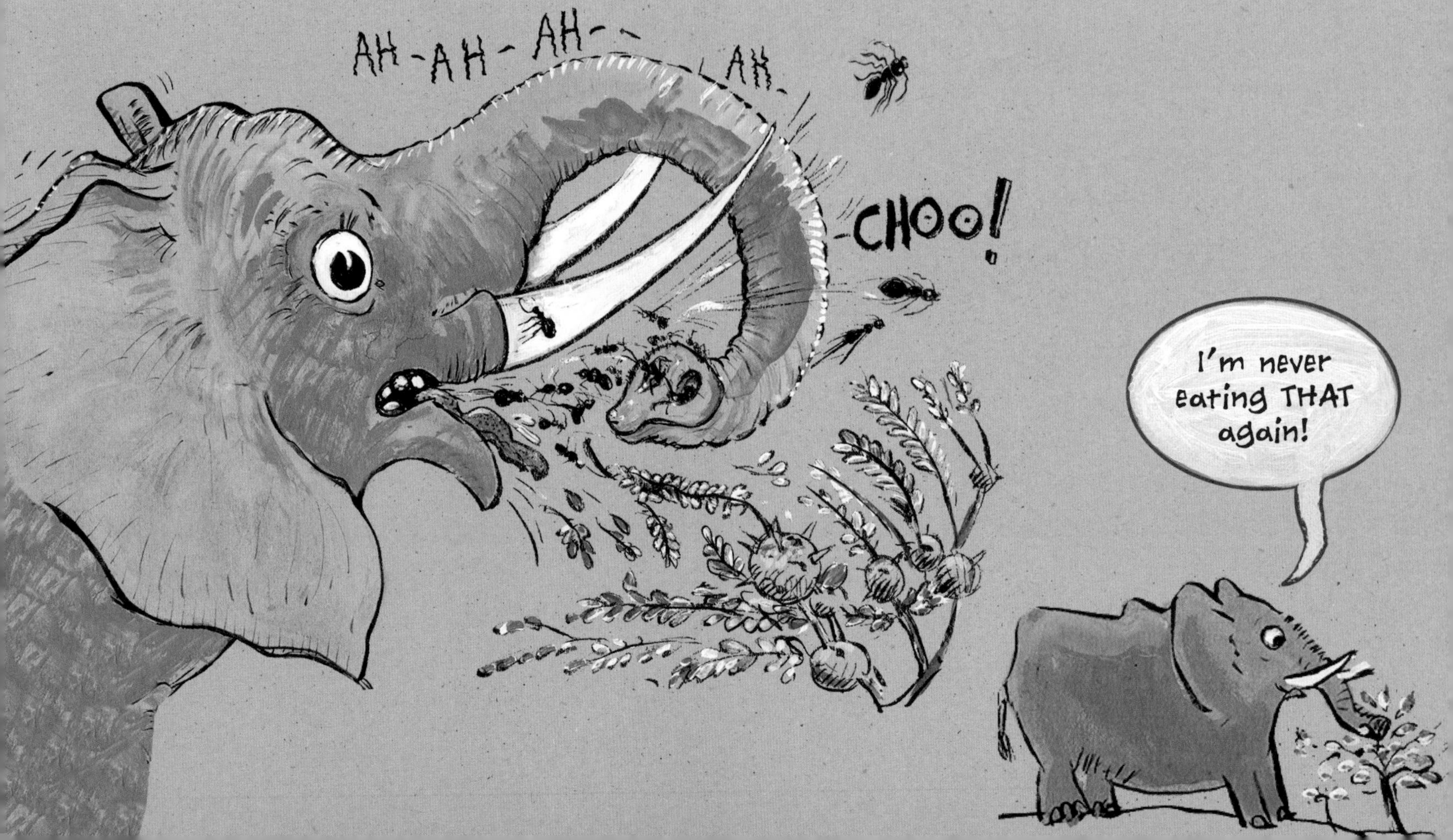
AH-AH-AH- -AH-CHOO!
I'm never eating THAT again!

TO PROTECT THE COLONY,

EXPLODING ANTS ACTUALLY EXPLODE!

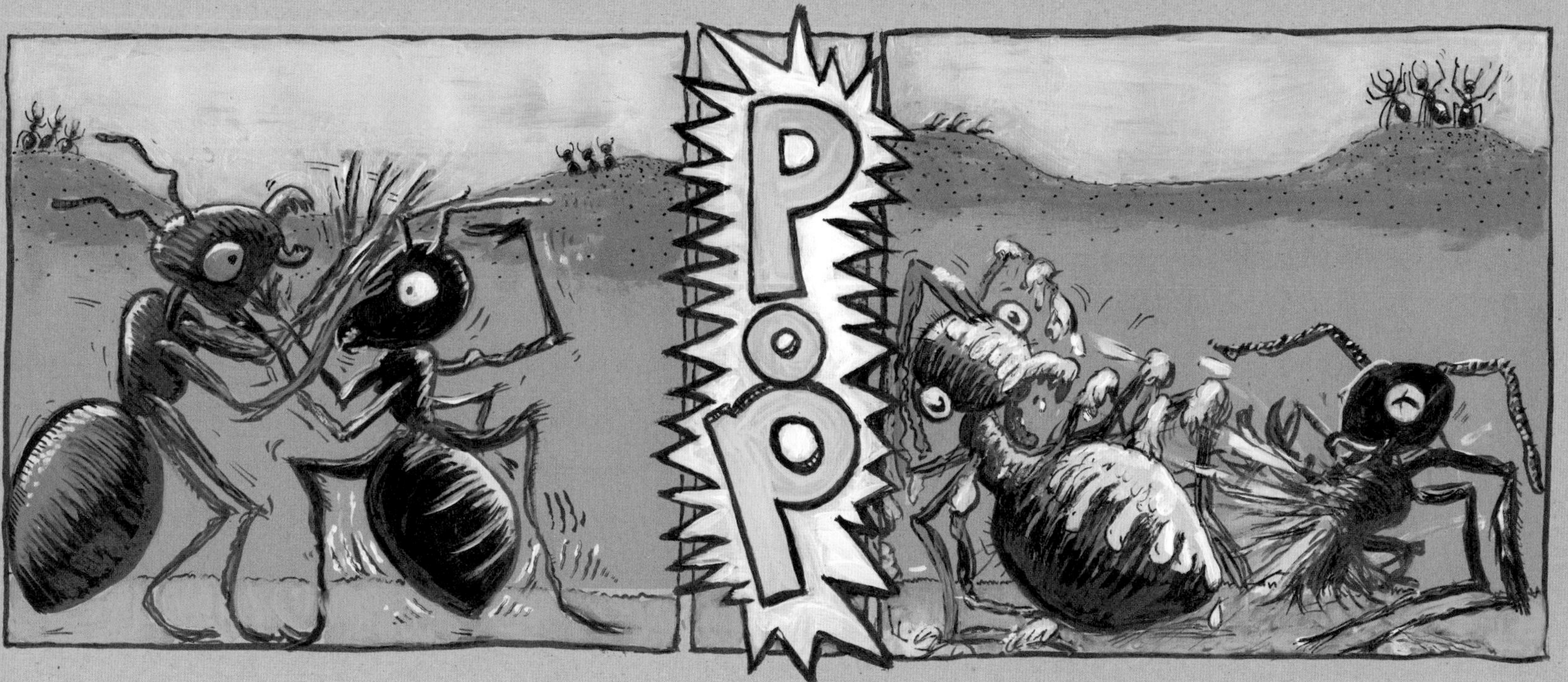
POP

THEY COVER THEIR ENEMY IN YELLOW GOO.

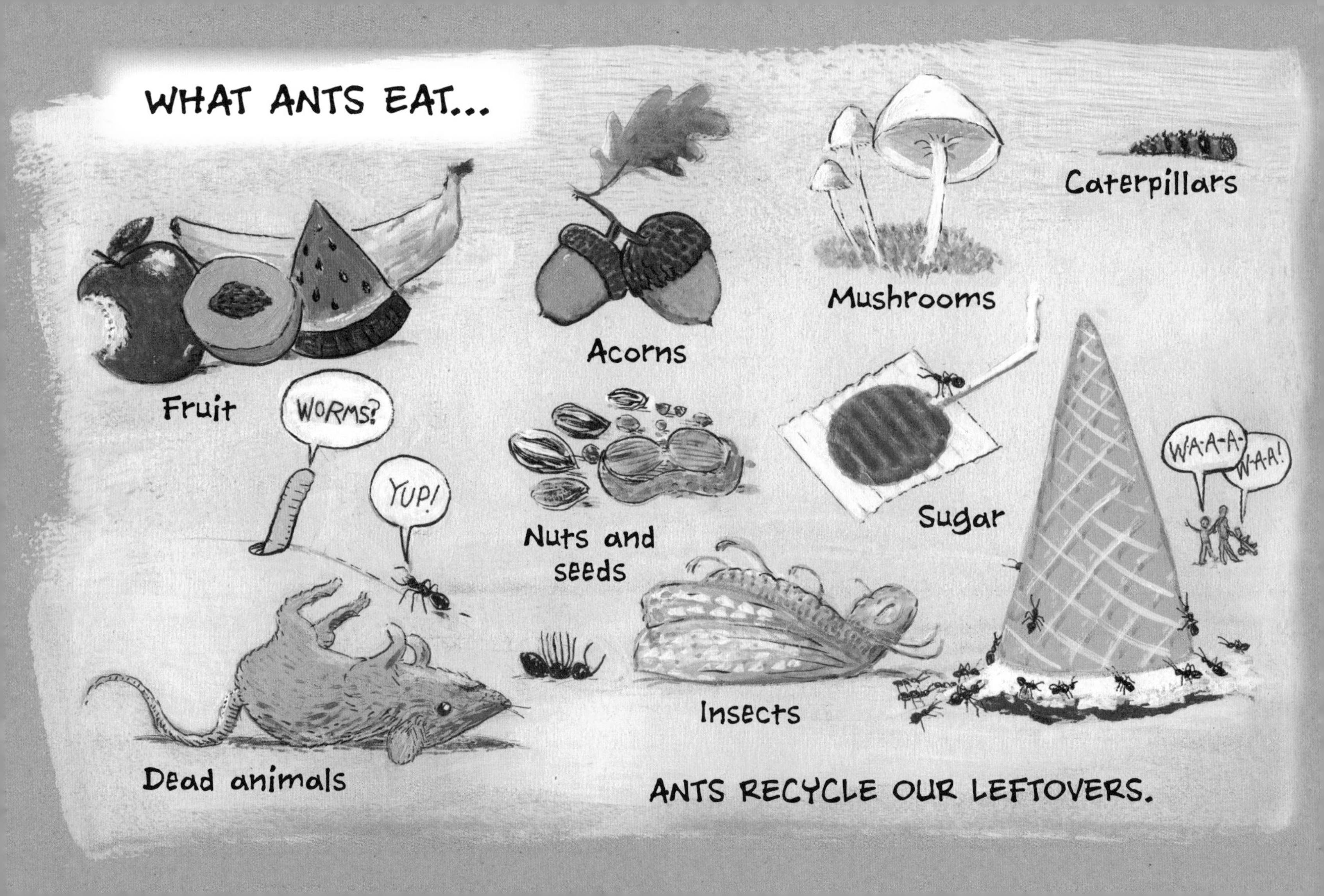
WHAT ANTS EAT...
Acorns
Mushrooms
Caterpillars
Fruit
WORMS?
YUP!
Nuts and seeds
Sugar
W-A-A-A-
W-A-A!
Insects
Dead animals
ANTS RECYCLE OUR LEFTOVERS.

WHAT EATS ANTS...

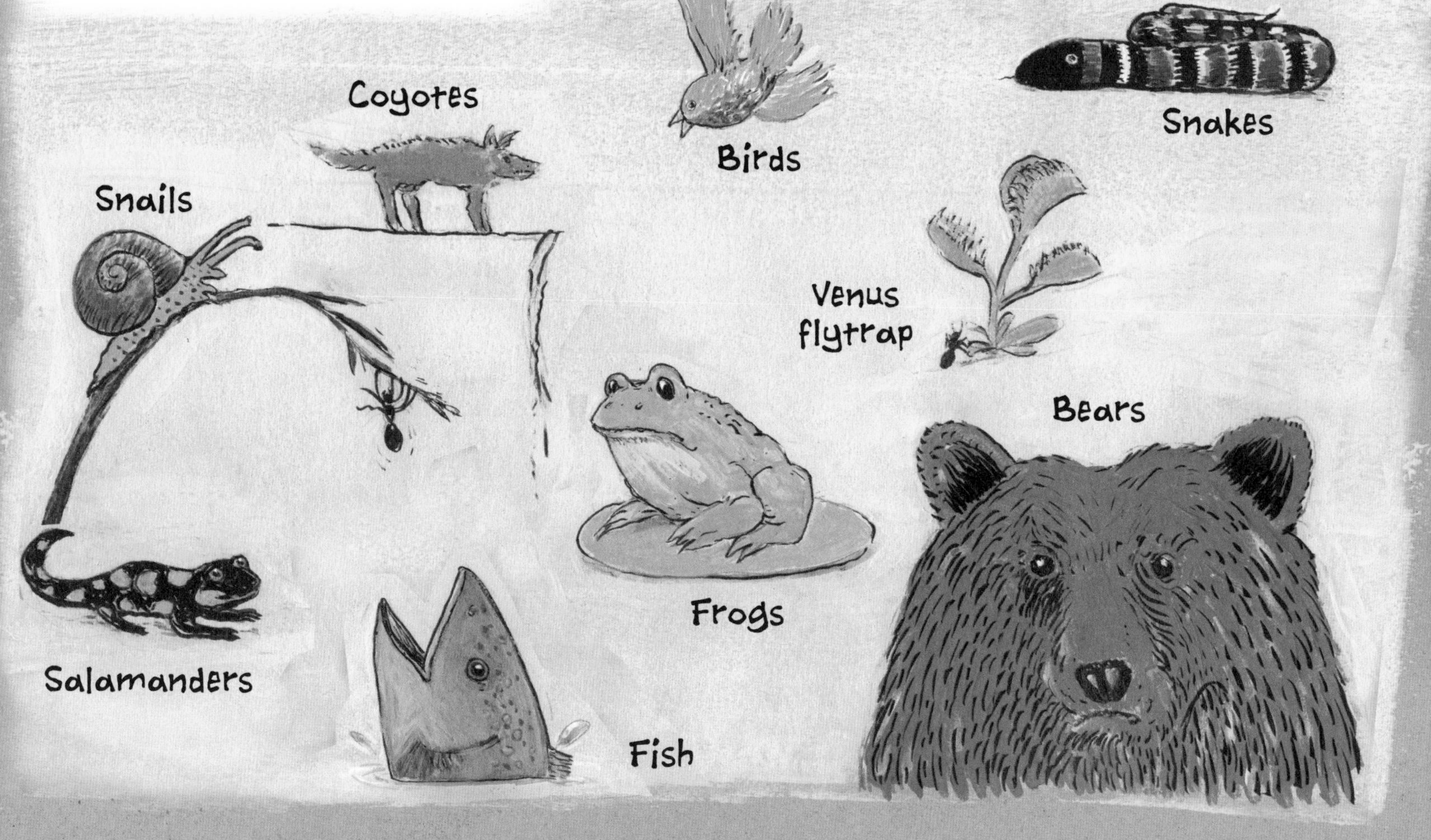
Coyotes
Birds
Snakes
Snails
Venus flytrap
Bears
Frogs
Salamanders
Fish

LET'S NOT FORGET ANTEATERS!

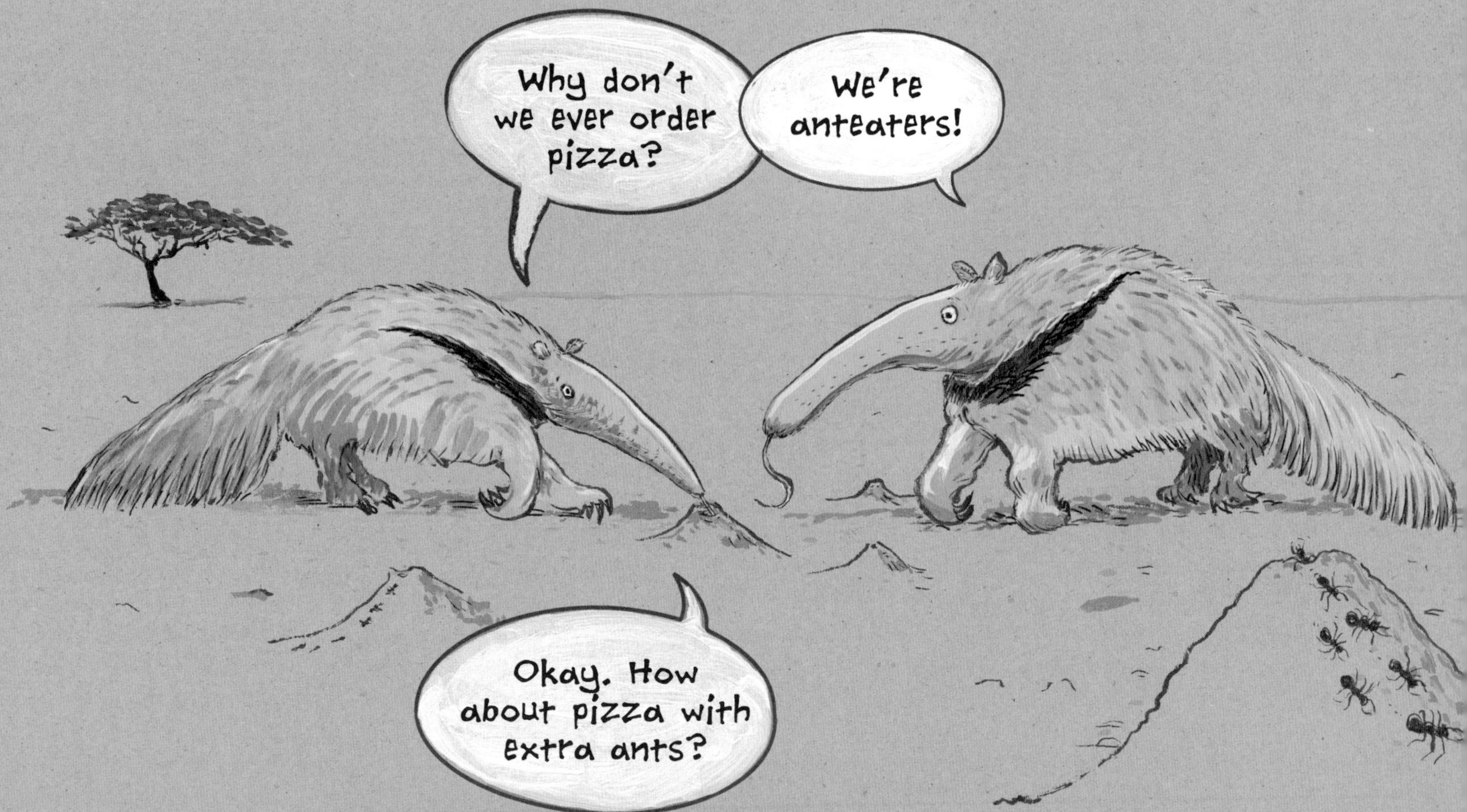
Why don't we ever order pizza?
We're anteaters!
Okay. How about pizza with extra ants?

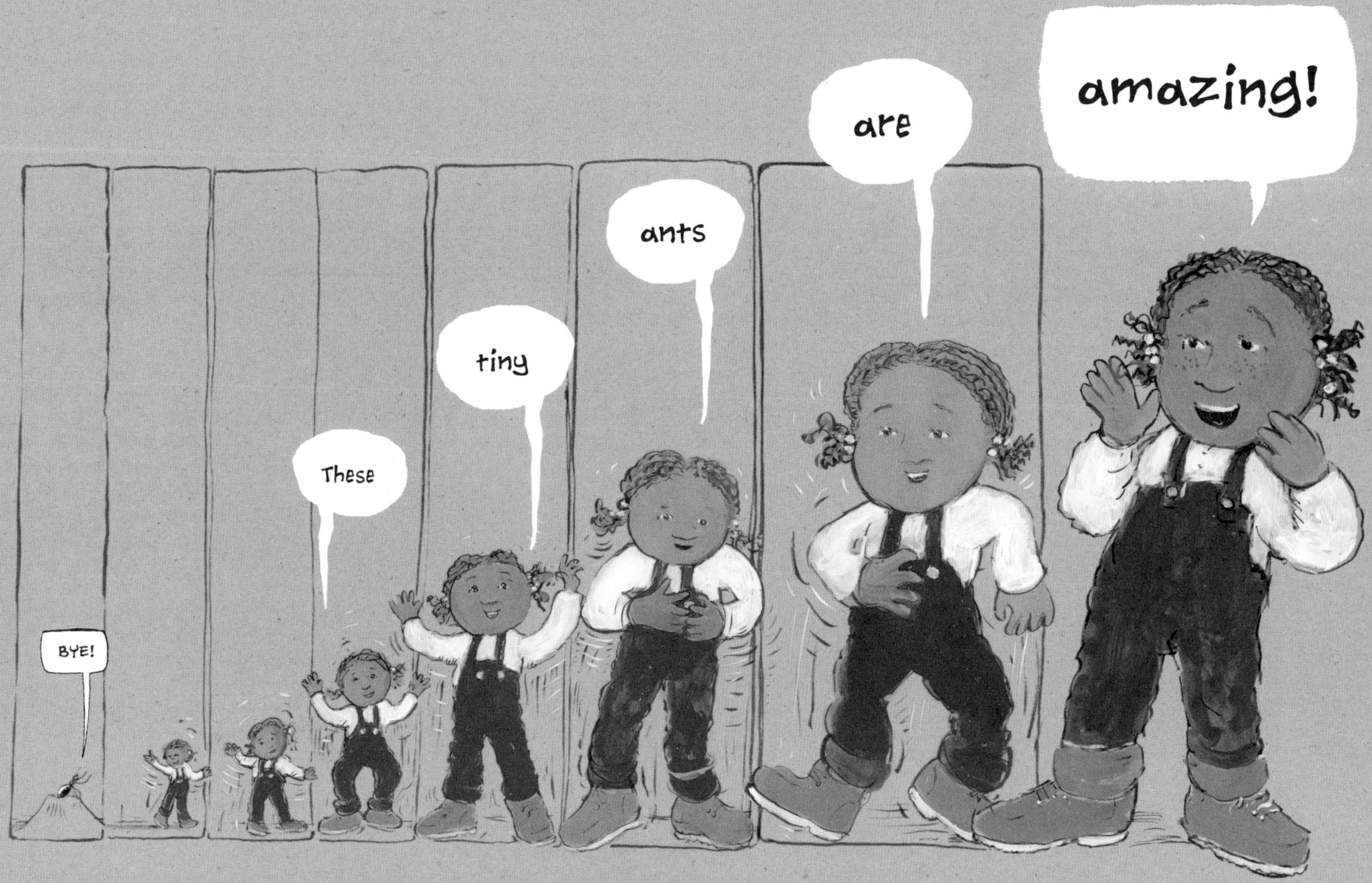
BYE!
These
tiny
ants
are
amazing!

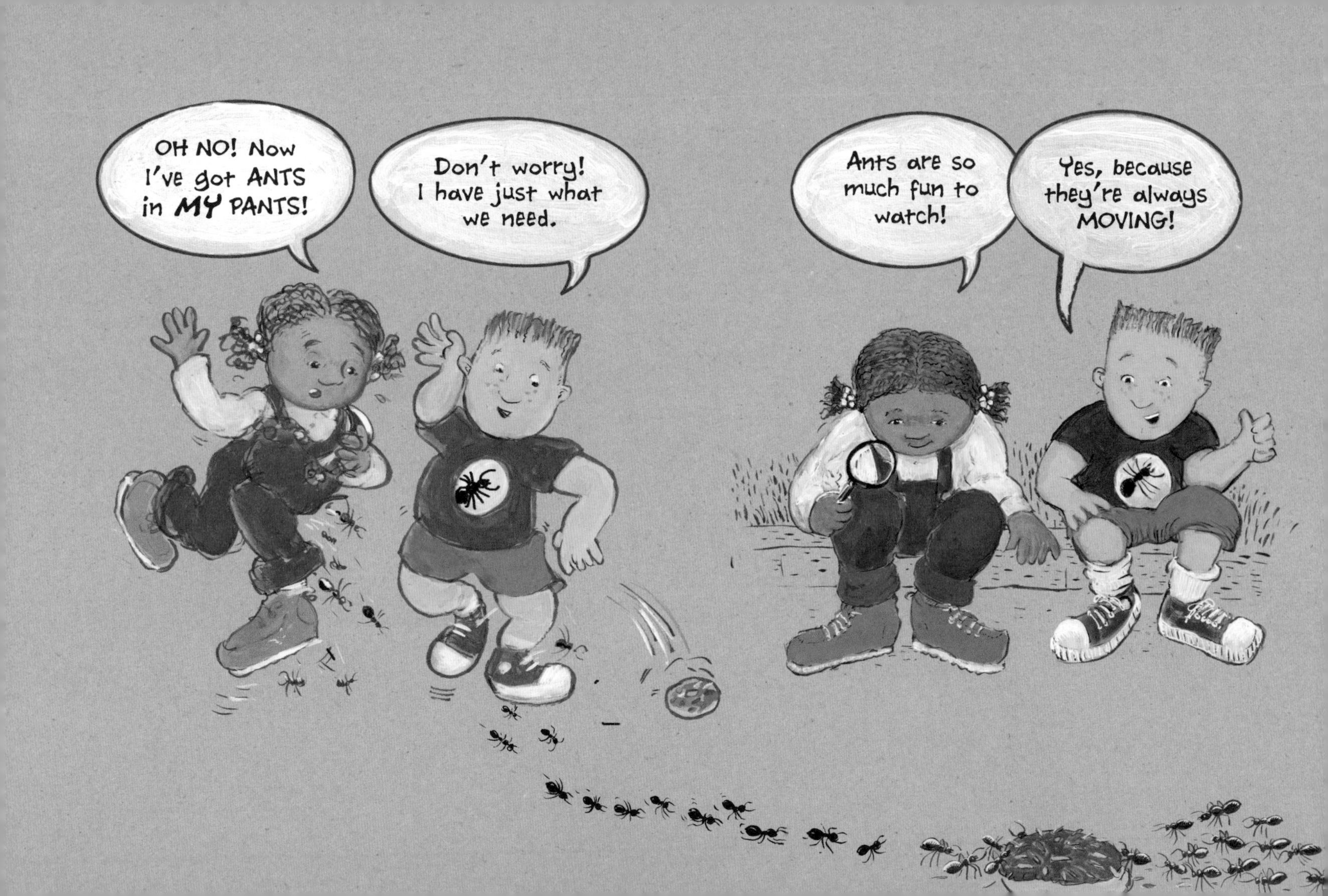
OH NO! Now I've got ANTS in MY PANTS!
Don't worry! I have just what we need.
Ants are so much fun to watch!
Yes, because they're always MOVING!